Birds of All Feathers underscores the importance of diversity and inclusion in driving employee engagement. It offers a holistic approach to diversity, encouraging the reader to see the importance of integrating it into all aspects of an organization, and highlighting its power to drive the bottom line when supported by leadership and principles.
BLAKE HUTCHESON, President and CEO, OMERS

Birds of All Feathers has become my essential guide to being a better employer. It's fearless, funny, engaging, refreshingly frank, and full of Bach's characteristic compassion and humanity. Come for the advice, stay for the stories of what it's like to work in the inclusion trenches.
MARGARET EATON, National CEO, Canadian Mental Health Association

Michael Bach challenges the notion that diversity and inclusion is no more than just "the right thing to do." By combining his considerable subject matter knowledge with instructive business cases, Bach has demonstrated how strategically critical it is to drive D&I purposefully in every type of organization.
JULIE O'MARA, President and Board Chair, The Centre for Global Inclusion

This should be required reading for any C-level leader looking to kick their organization's D&I into high gear. Bach's insights are brisk, instructive, and readily applicable across a spectrum of business models.
NIKKI HOLLAND, President and CEO, Jewish Federations of Canada – United Israel Appeal

Michael Bach is one of the leading architects for diversity and inclusion in North American workplaces. *Birds of All Feathers* is proof that he is still pushing the discourse forward with practical solutions and tactical guidance for navigating the constantly evolving D&I landscape to superlative strategic success.

RATNA OMIDVAR, Canadian Senator

This book will convince any leader that leveraging D&I fosters greater creativity and innovation—and that there are clear steps you can take to move your organization forward. It is an inspiring call to action, and a practical guide to successful diversity and inclusion.

ANDREW GRAHAM, Co-Founder & CEO, Borrowell

Birds of All Feathers proves that diversity and inclusion are connected to sustained success, no matter the size of your organization or the industry in which it operates. This book will equip you to explain why diversity and inclusion matter, and will help you pursue practical and meaningful action in your organization.

NORM SABAPATHY, Executive Vice President,
People, Cadillac Fairview Corporation

This book is a must-have for organizations that want to do D&I the right way. With his friendly and upbeat style, Bach guides readers through complex topics, using real-life examples to illustrate how you can navigate emotionally charged issues and situations.

NANCY WILSON, CEO, Canadian Women's Chamber of Commerce

BIRDS
OF ALL
FEATHERS

BIRDS OF ALL FEATHERS

Doing Diversity and Inclusion Right

MICHAEL BACH

PAGE TWO BOOKS

Cataloguing in publication information is available from
Library and Archives Canada.
ISBN 978-1-989603-40-6 (paperback/hardcover)
ISBN 978-1-989603-41-3 (ebook)

Every reasonable effort has been made to contact the
copyright holders for work reproduced in this book.

Some names and identifying details have been changed
to protect the privacy of individuals.

Page Two
www.pagetwo.com

Cover and interior design by Jennifer Lum
Printed and bound in Canada by Friesens
Distributed in Canada by Raincoast Books
Distributed in the US and internationally by Macmillan

22 23 24 25 26   6 5 4 3 2

www.michaelbach.com

This book is dedicated to my parents, Karen and Stephen, for showing me the right path; to my sister Cassandra, for always having my back; to my dear friend Kate, for always knowing when wine was appropriate; to all my wonderful colleagues at CCDI for your tireless efforts and commitment to the journey; to all diversity and inclusion professionals for doing the work that others ignore; and last but never least, to my husband, Mike, for always being by my side. This is a gift to my niece Sandy, in hopes that the world you have will be better.

CONTENTS

OPENING THOUGHTS

"Diversity" and "inclusion" have become buzzwords. They're used in casual conversation by CEOs and world leaders in the same way I use words like "chocolate" and ... "chocolate." Because I like chocolate. A lot. It's an issue I'm working through with my therapist. Stop judging me.

But what do these words mean and why do they matter? And why did you just pick up a book about them?

Historically, in most Western countries, we have taken a "social justice" approach to the diversity and inclusion conversation. That is, a straight, white, able-bodied man must lose so that a [insert underrepresented group here] may gain. However—and here's the revelation—that approach has never worked. And in my humble opinion, it never will. At best, the pace of change has been like coming in second in the race, just behind a glacier. The social justice approach requires said straight, white, able-bodied man to willingly surrender power. And why would he? There's zero incentive. This method requires a world where self-interest doesn't exist.

1

Please don't say, "But it's the right thing to do." That has got to be the most overused and misunderstood statement ever uttered. *Of course, it's the right thing to do!* How many people wake up in the morning and think, "Today, I'm going to do the wrong thing"? Thankfully, very few. However, statements like "it's the right thing to do" lead us to the slippery slope of "morals" and "values."

Why would anyone think morals and values are a slippery slope? Well, arguably, everyone has morals and values. *Everyone.* Totalitarian dictators have what they would call morals and values; they just happen to be somewhat out of line with *my* morals and values. Hence where the slope slips. If everyone on the planet lived by the same moral compass— assuming that compass was set to words like "respect" and "equity"—we'd live in a utopia. Everyone would think the same and, as such, we would all be moving in the same direction—which, ultimately, would mean we wouldn't need things like a criminal justice system, because no one would commit crimes. Meanwhile, back here on planet Reality...

We don't all think the same way. (Thank heaven for that. To paraphrase General George S. Patton, if everyone thinks the same way, no one is thinking.) Therefore, we don't all have the same morals and values. Some might think that I, as an openly gay man, have no morals or values. Take those Christians who might describe themselves as "Big F" Fundamentalists and who may believe that their morals and values are "right" and "just" while at the same time believing that all gay people are abominations and should be put to death.

Mark 12:31 says, "Love your neighbor as yourself. There is no commandment greater…" Is that sentence somehow confusing? How can people call themselves good Christians and have hate in their hearts? And yes, I did just quote the Bible and General Patton in the same paragraph.

Cutting short my brilliant (one-sided) argument, my point is that you can have a set of morals and values that *you* believe to be right and just, and the person standing beside you can have a completely contrary set of morals and values and believe that they too are right and just. That's why the slope is so slippery, and it's why we need to stop saying that diversity and inclusion is "the right thing to do." We need to talk about diversity and inclusion as being good for our countries. It's good for our organizations. And it's good for each of us.

So why am I writing a book about this? I assure you it's not to feed my rather healthy ego. After nearly two decades of working professionally in the field of diversity and inclusion in workplaces all over the world (not to mention a lifetime of community involvement), I can say with confidence that I have seen more organizations do diversity poorly than well. For all of the hype about D&I (which is how all the cool kids refer to diversity and inclusion), most people still don't get it. It hasn't become part of our DNA. My hope is that we can start to right the ship so that people truly understand what *I* believe is the right way to "do" diversity and inclusion.

This book is meant to accomplish two things. First, it's meant to clearly articulate the WIIFM, or *what's in it for me*. What's in it for our countries? What's in it for employers?

What's in it for individuals? And yes, there is something in it for each of us. Second, it's meant to be a how-to guide on D&I for employers.

Why is the primary focus on employers? Well, it's what I know and do. My career has been varied. I've worked for large and small private-sector employers, in multiple countries, as a political staffer; I've been self-employed; and I've worked in the nonprofit space. Through it all, I've watched how employers treat their people. The employment world is one I can speak to with "authority" (and I use that term *very* loosely). Plus, the majority of people in every country "work" in some way, so this is all about a really big market.

Why is the book called *Birds of All Feathers*, you might ask? Excellent question. Thanks for asking. It's a metaphor. Here's how it goes: All birds have feathers. (It's true. I Googled it.) The birds represent employees. Employees are people. People function, for the most part, in the same way: we breathe; we think; we feel. D&I is all about creating space in the nest for *all* people (you see what I did there? Birds... nest... Gimme a break! They can't all be winners). Anyway, the emphasis is on the word *all*. Everyone needs to be part of this conversation. It can't be about everyone *except* straight, white, able-bodied men. If it is, we're getting nowhere. So this book is about all birds, regardless of their feathers.

Birds of All Feathers is the culmination of a lifetime of observations. My hope is that people can learn from what I have lived and witnessed and, with a little nudge, start making decisions—using a diversity and inclusion lens—that are in the best interest of themselves, their organizations, and their country.

That isn't to say that individuals won't get something out of reading this book. You will definitely (hopefully, probably) glean some new information that will help you think differently about diversity and inclusion. Or, if nothing else, you'll have a good giggle.

And *yes, you can laugh*. Heck, I hope you laugh. I'm using all my good material in here. My grandma always told me I was really funny. Then again, she made some seriously questionable life decisions. I strongly subscribe to the belief that people learn more effectively when they're laughing. D&I can be a heavy, serious topic. I inject humor into my writing so that you'll absorb more of what you're reading. Feel free to LOL, even if it's not genuine and you're doing it just to make me feel better. I'll take it where I can get it.

This book is also written in the first person. I'm sharing *my* thoughts and beliefs based on *my* experiences. This isn't a journal, but it also isn't an academic textbook. Although I sprinkled research throughout this book to make you think I'm smart, it's mostly based on my lived experience— working in the trenches, helping employers create more inclusive workplaces.

The last thing I'll say is an important, quite serious point: I'm not going to talk about marginalization. I won't use words like "anti-racism" and "anti-oppression." Racism and oppression exist, and I believe these are incredibly important conversations that need to happen. I just don't think I'm the best person to talk about them. If you look at my picture at the back of the book, you'll notice that, although I'm dashingly handsome, I'm a dashingly handsome white man. Yes, I'm gay and live with an invisible disability, and I have faced significant discrimination in my life. Yet I'm still pale and male, which comes with a huge amount of privilege. I'm not the guy to talk about marginalization. There are so many people who are far better suited to tackle that topic. The last thing we need is another white guy mansplaining things like oppression and racism. What I will talk about is what I know—things that you can do to make your world a more inclusive place.

Reading this book is one thing, but it doesn't stop there. This topic is constantly evolving. As such, I've created a sharing space at **www.michaelbach.com** where you can join in the conversation about anything you read here. Visit this site whenever you want to know more, or when you want to share your thoughts on a particular topic. My goal is to create a space where all birds can gather to share and learn. (You see . . . I called you all birds. Get it? And the bird jokes continue! I'm kidding. That's the last one. You're welcome.)

D&I DEFINED

Let's start with some words. This *is* a book, after all. Every person who picks up this book will have some preconceived ideas about what diversity and inclusion is. It's only natural. You've been hearing these words for quite some time. But what do they *really* mean? In this chapter, I share with you my understanding of some of the more common terminology used, and specifically the vocabulary I use throughout the book. Even if you know these words intimately, you may find a new perspective. And I present them in a somewhat specific order, because they build on one another. It's important that your knowledge grows from the beginning, not from the middle. As such, I've ordered the words accordingly, to start you at the right place. So, here goes.

Representation

You may be wondering why "representation" is the first word I mention. It's because there's a bit of confusion about the difference between representation and diversity. Representation is part of diversity, but not the entirety of it.

The *Oxford Dictionary* defines "representation" as "the description or portrayal of someone or something in a particular way or as being of a certain nature."[1] Essentially, representation is what we can see. It's what we can count. Representation is part of the diversity and inclusion conversation in that it focuses on counting certain groups: women, racialized people or people of color, people with disabilities, and so on. When one thinks of representation, Affirmative Action (legislation in the United States) or Employment Equity (Canada's far more polite, far less powerful iteration) often come to mind. Representation does two things: First, it looks at people as one-dimensional characters (see the definition of "intersectionality" below); and second, it doesn't account for the complexity that diversity really encompasses.

Focusing on representation is a tick-box exercise. It's all about counting. It doesn't take into consideration the bigger picture of whether people feel included. You can focus on the number of people that you have from an underrepresented group, but if you don't focus on the bigger picture of ensuring those people feel included and valued, twice as many people from that underrepresented group will be going out the back door than coming in the front entrance.

Diversity

The *Oxford Dictionary* definition of "diversity" is "a range of different things."[2] The reality is that diversity is about everything that makes you unique. Representation is part of diversity: diversity *is* about women and racialized people and people with disabilities, and so on. It's also about education, family status, marital status, and so much more. Diversity goes beyond representation to recognize that everyone is diverse in some way.

In my work, I use a model that has been around for quite some time to help explain the complexity of diversity. Originally created by Marilyn Loden and Judy Rosener, it helps us understand that everyone is made up of a complex set of circumstances and experiences. The original "Diversity Wheel" first appeared in Loden and Rosener's 1990 book *Workforce America! Managing Employee Diversity as a Vital Resource*. Another version of the wheel was published in Loden's second book, *Implementing Diversity*. An adaptation of the diversity wheel appeared in *Diverse Teams at Work* by Lee Gardenswartz and Anita Rowe.[3] All this to say, it's a model that's been around for a long time. It's tried-and-true. I subsequently adapted the model for my own illustrative purposes.

The model is made up of four layers, or dimensions, of the human condition—global, organizational, external, and internal. It centers on each person's personality, which is made up of their likes, dislikes, values, and beliefs. The model shows how a multitude of factors—be they internal

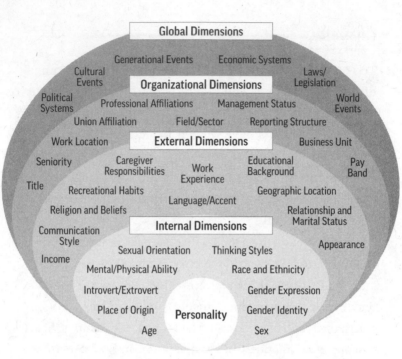

or external to you—can influence your personality. You will have significant control over some things, such as your caregiver responsibilities and geographic location, but little to no control over others, such as generational events or economic systems—even though they affect your personality and how you see and experience the world.

While the word "diversity" gets thrown around frequently, as you can see, it's quite complicated. Sometimes we hear employers say, "We need to hire more diverse people." My immediate response is, "What do you mean by 'diverse' people?" I push them to be honest about what they're talking about. "Diversity" is often code for people of color, or Indigenous people, or some other underrepresented group. The thing to keep in mind is that when you say "diversity," you're talking about everyone. Break the code!

Inclusion

Andrés Tapias wrote in his book *The Inclusion Paradox: The Post Obama Era and the Transformation of Global Diversity*: "Diversity is the mix. Inclusion is getting the mix to work well together."[4] Steve Robbins, a diversity and inclusion consultant in the United States (whom I have had the pleasure of studying with), says, "Diversity has sometimes been about counting people. Inclusion is about making people count."[5] And there are more catchy slogans. Lots more! Whichever catchphrase you prefer, the point is clear: diversity is not where employers struggle. Inclusion is.

Imagine a person joins an organization only to find they're the sole black person working there. What if people stare? What if people get quiet when they walk into the lunchroom? What if some super-friendly, well-meaning person touches their hair without asking? People may make assumptions about them—they're good at sports and music, but their work ethic is described as lazy. They just want to do their job, but everyone else is focused on one thing—the color of their skin. How long do you think that person is going to last?

You can replace "black person" with any underrepresented group and the example will still work. The problem isn't the lack of diversity—it's the lack of inclusion. Inclusion is about taking all the unique characteristics that people bring with them to work and making sure you have a workplace where everyone can succeed because of, and in spite of, those unique qualities.

Diversity and Inclusion

There is a great deal of debate about the order of these words. Is it diversity and inclusion? Inclusion and diversity? Inclusion or inclusivity? Maybe we should just talk about inclusion and stop talking about diversity altogether? To this I say... who cares.

There is a movement afoot to abandon the word "diversity" because some people feel it's become too stigmatized, but I completely disagree with this approach. It's not the word's fault. It's how we use the word. Suggesting the word is the problem is like suggesting the *word* "chocolate" is to blame for my pants being too tight. It's not the word. It's the chocolate (and my complete lack of self-control). Diversity and inclusion go together like peanut butter and chocolate, or gin and tonic. You can't have one without the other. Well, I suppose that's not accurate, but let's stay on point.

Just focusing on diversity ignores the fact that you need to make sure everyone works well together. You can have a diverse workforce but incredibly low productivity because those "diverse people" don't feel like they belong. Conversely, simply focusing on inclusion runs the risk of forgetting who you're trying to include in the first place. Today's focus on diversity and inclusion stems from the civil rights movement and the need to ensure that everyone can succeed in society. You can have an incredibly inclusive workplace but have little difference among your staff.

Human Rights

The United Nations Office of the High Commissioner on Human Rights defines "human rights" as: "inherent to all human beings, whatever our nationality, place of residence, sex, national or ethnic origin, color, religion, language, or any other status. We are all equally entitled to our human rights without discrimination. These rights are all interrelated, interdependent and indivisible."[6]

In most Western countries, we have some form of human rights legislation. Although there can be vast differences in each country's laws, these legislations prohibit discrimination against people on protected grounds in protected social areas. As an example, in Ontario, Canada, these areas include:

- Accommodation (housing)
- Contracts
- Employment
- Goods, services, and facilities
- Membership in trade unions or professional associations

There is a direct connection between diversity and inclusion and human rights broadly, but this type of language is used more in the public sector. In my opinion, when we speak about human rights, we are often speaking about diversity and inclusion.

Equity

"Equity" is defined as "the quality of being fair and impartial."[7] Equity is about leveling the playing field so that everyone has the opportunity to succeed.

Equality versus Equity

There is some misunderstanding about the difference between "equality" and "equity." Equality means treating two people exactly the same. Equity means treating each person appropriately, according to what they need or deserve.

Consider the example of men and women as it relates to human reproduction. In heterosexual relationships between cisgender people (people whose identity and gender correspond with the sex they were assigned at birth), if the couple chooses to conceive, generally speaking, both the man and woman participate. However, that's where equality stops. The man is engaged for about three minutes (don't kid yourself— you know that's generous), but the woman is in it for the long haul—nine months of gestation followed by a period of healing, and so much more. So how can we possibly treat men and women the same?

The difference between these two terms was succinctly summarized in a tweet by Dr. Naheed Dosani in 2014: "Equality is giving everyone a shoe. Equity is giving everyone a shoe that fits."[8]

Human Rights and Equity

Sometimes, particularly in the public service sector (schools, hospitals, and so on), you'll hear the phrase "human rights and equity." For the purposes of this book, I'll use human rights and equity interchangeably with diversity and inclusion.

Accessibility

"Accessibility" is generally used in conjunction with access for people with disabilities. The definition of the word is "the quality of being able to be reached or entered."[9] Accessibility is often forgotten when speaking about diversity and inclusion, but it is the missing link. You can have the most diverse workforce and the most inclusive workplace, but if anyone experiences barriers to access—be they physical, institutional, societal, or the like—then you haven't ensured inclusion for all.

There are the obvious barriers: steps to get into a building, a speech that doesn't include a sign language interpreter, not having Braille on signs, and so on. But there are many other, less apparent barriers to access. Consider this: if you do not have English, French, Spanish, German, or Italian as a primary language, accessing services in most Western countries can be very difficult. If your primary language is Vietnamese and you are the victim of a crime in, say, any city in Canada, language could present a significant barrier when you are interacting with the police, and this may result in the perpetrator going free.

And yes (before you think it), it should be the case that everyone who calls a country home has a certain level of proficiency in the dominant language of that country. That said, as an example, approximately 25 percent of newcomers to Canada each year come through the Family Class Sponsorship Program or the Family Reunification Program; and around 11 percent come as refugees (most Western countries have similar categories and percentages). These classes of immigration are similar in other countries and tend to have a lower standard for language proficiency, which means that hundreds of thousands of newcomers each year *may* have a lower level of proficiency in your official language. To ensure newcomers can access services (while they're building proficiency in the dominant language), it's imperative that service providers take alternate languages into consideration in the provision of their services.

Accommodation

This is another "A" word that is often connected to people with disabilities but has far more reach. "Accommodation" is defined as "a convenient arrangement; a settlement or compromise."[10] While I don't love the definition (arguably little is "convenient" about accommodation), it is clear that accommodation relates to equity: treating each person appropriately, according to what they need and/or deserve.

Similar to accessibility, when we think about accommodation, we typically think of things like ramps into buildings or Braille on signs. However, accommodation encompasses a multitude of things: flexible work arrangements, smoke breaks, aerodynamic keyboards, and so on. Everything in life is an accommodation for someone.

Intersectionality

The word "intersectionality" has been around for a long time, but from a diversity and inclusion perspective, it was coined in 1989 by Kimberlé Crenshaw in a paper focused on the disparities faced by African-American women.[11] Only recently has the term come into vogue, as it helps us understand the complexity of diversity. Crenshaw's definition of intersectionality is "the interconnected nature of social categorizations such as race, class, and gender as they apply to a given individual or group, regarded as creating overlapping and interdependent systems of discrimination or disadvantage."

To provide a Canadian example, I turn to a report from the Canadian Research Institute for the Advancement of Women called *Everyone Belongs: A Toolkit for Applying Intersectionality*. The report shows the intersections of sex, education, and immigrant status using data from Statistics Canada on the median income of Canadians from 2005.

Canadian-born men with a university education had the highest median income of $62,566. Conversely, women without a university education who had recently immigrated to Canada had the lowest median income of $14,233. Consistently, men within each category (Canadian-born, immigrant, recent immigrant) earned higher incomes than women in the same groups; and women with longer histories in Canada outearned newer arrivals.[12] While this is relatively old data, it shows us that we can't think of *all* women as one group. Mitigating factors and variables need to be considered. Examining intersectionality helps us better understand some of the incongruities of individual groups by not thinking of each as a one-dimensional unit.

Visible Minorities, Racialized People, People of Color

Each country has its own descriptors and definitions (often defined and used in legislation) of what constitutes a minority as it relates to ethnocultural identity. In Canada, the term "visible minority" is used, particularly in the Employment Equity Act. However, in February 2007 the United Nations Committee on the Elimination of Racial Discrimination issued a comment suggesting the phrase "visible minority" itself may be discriminatory.[13] To my knowledge, Canada is the only country that uses the phrase. So, yeah, the UN was coming for Canada.

The phrase dates back to 1984 and the creation of the Employment Equity Act and describes "persons, other than

Aboriginal Peoples, who are non-Caucasian in race or non-white in color."[14] The qualifier "visible" was included with "minority" to distinguish newer immigrant minorities from Indigenous Peoples and other minority groups determined by language (French versus English) and religion (Catholics versus Protestants), which are predominantly "invisible" traits. That said, the term is quite dated, and outside of usage by Statistics Canada and other government bodies, it's not used often.

Many in the diversity and inclusion field have shifted to the term "racialized people." Although not perfect, the term has become generally acceptable to use in place of visible minority. The term "people of color" is used in the United States and Australia to describe the same group—that is, anyone who isn't white—particularly in legislation related to affirmative action and equal employment opportunity. But that term has a long history that isn't pretty. *The American Heritage Guide to Contemporary Usage and Style* cites usage of "people of color" in the United States dating back to 1796, to refer to light-skinned people of mixed African and European heritage who were free, as opposed to American slaves, who were of Afro-Caribbean descent.

In the United Kingdom, the term BAME—black, Asian, and minority ethnic—is used by the Office for National Statistics. I'm not sure how I feel about that one. Isn't referring to someone as a "minority ethnic" just as bad as a visible minority? What if they aren't actually a minority?

This is all to say that determining the correct terms is an ongoing conversation. Generally speaking, I don't like any of them because it continues to "other" people by saying you're either white or you're something else. By the time this book is published, the words may have changed again. Stay tuned.

Handicapped versus Person with a Disability

Using the word "handicapped" to describe a person living with a disability is viewed as quite offensive. As a human condition, the word "disabled" has become the norm. It is, however, acceptable (and better) to use the terms "person with a disability" or "person living with a disability" rather than "disabled" or "disabled person."

SWAM

The acronym SWAM is one that, I confess, I am responsible for creating. In speaking at the 2008 Conference Board of Canada's Workplace Diversity and Inclusiveness Forum, I gave a speech entitled "Diversity and the Straight White Able-bodied Man: Putting the Inclusion in Diversity and Inclusion."[15] The purpose was to speak about the one group that has traditionally been left out of the diversity conversation. Without thinking about it, I referred to said Straight White Able-bodied Man as a SWAM (pronounced like "swan" with an *m*, as opposed to the past tense of swim). Since then, the term SWAM has been cropping up all over the place.[16] So ... you're welcome.

Equity-Seeking Groups

An equity-seeking group is any group of individuals who are (or feel they are) in the minority in some way and are seeking equity within a particular circumstance. For example, women are an equity-seeking group in the engineering profession because women account for only around 25 percent of engineering degrees awarded each year. Equity-seeking groups exist anywhere there is a disparity between groups.

LGBTQ2+

The abbreviation LGBTQ2+ stands for lesbian, gay, bisexual, trans-identified, queer, two-spirit. The + symbol is *intended* to represent any diverse sexuality or gender that people self-identify with that may not be represented in the other letters. The "real" abbreviation is significantly longer and attempts to include more sexualities and genders, but for the purposes of this book, I will use the shorter version. I put "real" in quotes above because there are several versions of the abbreviation. If you want to know more, you can look at the *Comprehensive* List of LGBTQ+ Vocabulary Definitions.*[17] It's a great read with lots of interesting information to help educate you and your people on the complexity of sexual and gender identities.

Sex, Sexual Orientation, Gender Identity, and Gender Expression

So much confusion exists about the differences between sex, sexual orientation, gender identity, and gender expression. I was interviewed not too long ago, and the reporter struggled with the idea that sexuality and gender have nothing to do with one another. Oh, if only there were a way to learn about this... if only she had Google...

I have seen no better resource on the topic than the website ItsPronouncedMetrosexual.com. It has brilliant resources on the topic, including a model called the Genderbread Person, which clearly explains the differences between identity, attraction, expression, and sex.[18] But let me break it down for you as simply as I can: "Sex" refers to our biology, the physical characteristics that we're born with. "Sexual orientation" refers to who you are sexually or romantically attracted to. "Gender identity" refers to what gender you identify with, regardless of your biological sex. "Gender expression" refers to how you present yourself, through things like the way you dress and how you act.

The most important point: sex, sexual orientation, gender identity, and gender expression are four completely separate things, and although they're interrelated, they are not interdependent. You can be assigned male at birth, be gay, identify as gender nonconforming (meaning you don't follow the stereotypes about how a person of your sex should act or look), and present as a man. Insert head explosion emoji.

Diversity Fatigue

You're going to hear this one quite a bit—it's so important that I wrote a whole chapter on it. I started using this phrase about a decade ago as I watched a previous employer start to run into trouble on its D&I journey. "Diversity fatigue" means exactly what you might think: tired of diversity. This exhaustion sets in when an organization has been on its D&I journey for some time and it just starts to run out of steam with trying to realize its goals. This is pretty common, and I've seen it in many organizations.

Reverse Discrimination

My good friends at the *Oxford Dictionary* define "reverse discrimination," in the context of the allocation of resources or employment, as "the practice or policy of favoring individuals belonging to groups known to have been discriminated against previously; positive discrimination."[19]

In short, it's a practice of selecting a candidate because of a personal characteristic (such as women, people of color, and so on) and not because of their ability to do the job.

I disagree with this term completely. There's no such things as *reverse* discrimination. It's just discrimination. If you are hiring someone and you select a candidate because of a characteristic other than their ability to do the job, then you're discriminating against the other candidates. It doesn't matter whom you're discriminating against, it's still discrimination.

Bona Fide Occupational Requirement

You're going to hear this term again in the pages to come. A "bona fide occupational requirement," or BFOR, is an attribute that employers are allowed to consider when deciding on the hiring and retention of employees. The law in Canada regarding BFORs was considered in a 1985 court case between CN Railway and one of its employees, K.S. Bhinder, a Sikh, whose religion requires that he wear a turban. Bhinder lost his challenge of the CN policy that required him to wear a hard hat.[20]

In essence, a BFOR is a requirement of a job that can be defended as an absolute must-have. If you work in a bilingual call center, a BFOR might be that you have a certain level of both English and another language. To drive a bus, a BFOR would be that you have a certain class of driver's license. Sometimes, a BFOR may go against a person's human rights as protected under law and still be acceptable, as it was in Bhinder's case.[21]

Privilege

The last word in our little lexicon is a tough one. "Privilege." Normally I don't speak much about privilege unless it's to acknowledge and talk about my own privilege as a white man. That said, there is no way I can write a book on diversity and inclusion without acknowledging the proverbial pink elephant. The definition of the word is "a special right, advantage, or immunity granted or available only to a particular person or group of people."[22] There are multiple types of privilege in a Western context: male privilege, white privilege, straight privilege, able-bodied privilege, and so on. Any group that receives preferential treatment because of a specific characteristic is experiencing privilege. Let me give you an example.

Years ago, I was traveling from Toronto, Ontario, to a small community in the United States with a colleague of South Asian heritage. To get to the town, we had to travel on a very small plane, one that had eighteen seats in total. At the time, it was a policy of airport security to "randomly" search two people from every outbound flight. We were both wearing suits and both spoke English as a first language. The only real difference between us was that my skin is white and my colleague's is brown. I passed through screening without being stopped. My colleague was "randomly selected" to be searched. They were the only person of color on the flight. While it may have been truly random, it was, at the very least, a little suspect.

In this instance, because of the color of my skin, I experienced a privilege that was not afforded my colleague. Although this may seem like a small inconvenience, if you experienced something like it every day of your life, it would be similar to death by a thousand paper cuts. Not to mention the risk associated with the potential assumptions that were made about my colleague, which were not made about me.

You may be thinking that what I've described is a simple security practice, but consider this. According to the website

Statista, in the United States between 1982 and 2020, there were 118 mass shootings.[23] Of those, 64 were committed by white shooters, with the next largest group being black shooters at 20. Only eight shooters were of Asian descent. The disparity between groups is significant. Is it still a good security practice to target people because of the color of their skin? Or are we making assumptions and applying privilege where it doesn't belong?

Now, before you say, "I don't have privilege," consider a few examples that may make you think differently:

- Have you ever been stopped by police because they thought you couldn't afford the car you were driving simply because of how you looked? (white privilege, age privilege)

- Have you ever worried about how you were going to afford to eat? (socioeconomic privilege)

- Have you ever been worried about walking home alone at night out of a fear for your safety? (male privilege)

- Have you been denied employment or service because of your perceived sexual orientation? (straight privilege)

- Do you identify as male or female? (gender privilege)

- Have you ever not been able to enter a building because of a step or lack of barrier-free access? (able-bodied privilege)

The point is not to make you feel bad for your privilege but to make you aware of it. Many people have privilege, and it's not exclusive to SWAMs. Oftentimes, you may not even be aware that you're receiving privilege. However, the catch about privilege is that you have absolutely no choice in the matter. Privilege is assigned to you and exists, whether you like it or not. The question is, what do you do with it?

2

THE MODELS OF
DIVERSITY AND INCLUSION

Believe it or not, there are two models of diversity and inclusion: the social justice model and the creativity and innovation model. I know, I was shocked too. Here's another surprise: one of them works; the other doesn't. And before I get hate mail, I will make my argument about why the social justice model doesn't work.

Think of the difference between the social justice and creativity and innovation models like the difference between using a printed map and using a mapping app on your phone. (Don't laugh! My father still uses a printed map to navigate.) The printed map doesn't have any consideration for the daily changes on roads and to routes. Like a printed map, the social justice model is inherently dated. A mapping app, on the other hand, can tell you what traffic is like at any given time of any day, where roadwork is being done, and the best detour to avoid the scene of an accident. If you'll forgive the rhyme, map apps adapt to the ever-changing landscape, as does the creativity and innovation model.

Understanding these two models is important because although you might think you're focused on creativity and innovation, your actions may be more aligned to social justice.

Social Justice Model

Most of us are more familiar with the social justice model of D&I. The trusty *Oxford* defines "social justice" as "justice in terms of the distribution of wealth, opportunities, and privileges within a society."[1] That sounds ideal, but it also sounds like something else: socialism. In North America, we don't live in a socialist society, whether we want to or not. Aspects of our societies are socialist in nature (the Canadian medical system, as an example), but we live in a capitalist society. At best, most Western cultures are a hybrid of capitalism and socialism, but it's really big *C*, little *s*.

As I mentioned at the opening of this book, from a D&I perspective, the social justice model looks like: "SWAM must lose for [insert underrepresented group here] to gain." An article from the National Association of Independent Schools elaborates on this theme, stating that using a social justice framework to guide D&I efforts can help address issues of injustice in our society, especially where access and marginalization are concerned.[2] To be "Krystle Carrington" clear,

I agree with what the article's author, Jesse Gillispie, is saying. However, based on my experience, I don't believe that
approach is ever going to work, because of the imperative to
"address issues of injustice." For example, let's look at one big
issue of injustice: slavery. (Who said this book wasn't going
to be fun?!)

Since you and I have never owned slaves, is it our
responsibility to make reparations for slavery? Yes and no: No,
we shouldn't feel guilty for slavery because we weren't there.
Slavery was bad—it's among the worst things that have happened in history—but we have zero personal responsibility
for the act of slavery, making it very difficult to take personal
ownership of that terrible injustice. But yes, it is our responsibility in that we must be accountable for fixing the mess our
ancestors made. The trauma of slavery is still ever-present in
socicty today, and doing nothing about it produces nothing
new. So don't feel bad about it, but do something to make
amends, such as working to address issues of poverty within
black communities. Slavery is partly to blame for the dispro-
portionate socioeconomic disparity that exists within many
black communities. If employers were focused on addressing
such disparities, they would be working to address the histor-
ical burden of slavery.

Let me give you another, more personal example. My
maternal grandmother, Doris Kennedy, was a wonderful
woman. She was the matriarch of our family, lived to ninety-
eight years old, and was one of my most favorite people in
the world. She was also a racist. I'm not saying that to be

dramatic, and I'm not saying it to tarnish her name. She simply was racist.

Oxford defines a racist as "a person who shows or feels discrimination or prejudice against people of other races, or who believes that a particular race is superior to another."[3] Yeah, that was Doris. She would often describe any people who didn't appear to be Caucasian as "Chinamen." She wasn't terribly discerning. Men, women, black, East Asian, South Asian: all Chinamen.

Am I responsible for her actions? No, absolutely not. Doris was responsible for herself, and it's not up to me to apologize to every person she referred to as a Chinaman. Thankfully, my mother broke the cycle of bias and I grew up with a different understanding of ethnocultural identity. I don't condone Doris's actions, and in fact I condemn them. But the sins of the father (or grandmother) are not passed to the child.

The social justice model of diversity and inclusion requires all of us to take responsibility for the sins of our ancestors, and it also assumes we know the sins exist. It assumes we don't have our own set of biases that affect our decision-making processes. It also requires said straight, white, able-bodied men to give up power, willingly. The social justice model has not been effective in the past sixty-plus years because it requires the group in power—often, if not always, SWAMs—to have zero self-interest and to surrender their positions of power, simply because "it's the right thing to do."

If it's the right thing to do, it raises the question, why haven't we done it already? As I mentioned in my Opening

Thoughts, we haven't done it because we do not have a consistent understanding of what the right thing to do actually is. That it's the right thing to do will never be enough incentive to move the needle. What will be is a consistent understanding of why doing the "right thing" benefits everyone and how to do it.

It's sad to say, but the social justice model is not going to work, or at least it's not going to work at an acceptable pace. I want to see change in my lifetime. And that will require a different model.

Creativity and Innovation Model

Let's consider D&I through the lens of creativity and innovation. The world is in a period of rapid change. The amount of data on the planet doubles every two years, a result of our ever-increasing dependence on all things electronic.[4] Along with this situation comes an increasing number of challenges to be addressed. To develop solutions to the problems we're facing, we need to increase creativity and innovation. We simply need more and *different* ideas. Ideas are the solutions to problems. Diversity is the *means* to new and different ideas. I can't take credit for the concept of diversity being the means of creativity and innovation. Dr. Steve Robbins introduced this idea to me about ten years ago.

Let's look at a simplistic example that proves the point: talent shortage. In North America, many industries, such as manufacturing and technology, face significant talent shortages. There aren't enough people to fill the available jobs.

According to research by Korn Ferry, by 2030 we can expect a global talent deficit of 85.2 million workers, resulting in $8.452 trillion in unrealized annual revenue.[5] A number of factors contribute to the shortage: low birth rates over thirty years, extreme growth, shifts in the types of work, and so on. Regardless of "why" the deficit exists, employers are still struggling to find the "who" to do the work.

The answer to the problem is diversity and inclusion. Well, the answer is actually just "diversity," but if you don't add in inclusion, you won't be successful with the diversity you bring in. More on that to come.

Employers have realized that to address the shortage, they need to attract anyone and everyone with the skills their organizations need—and to retain people, they must create workplaces where anyone and everyone can succeed. Long gone are the days when it was okay to have a workforce dominated by SWAMs—because employers can't afford to rely exclusively on one demographic group as a pipeline of talent.

Look at technology as an example. Korn Ferry's research predicted that by 2020 (aka now), the technology, media, and telecommunications (TMT) industries may be short more than 1.1 million skilled workers globally. Now combine that fact with another: Among the twenty countries that Korn Ferry studied, only India is expected to see a talent surplus, because of its growing population of post-secondary educated people. Within the next decade, India's pool of college-educated talent is projected to rise by more than forty-five million. So, where would a be good place to find available talent?

Employers need to attract from the widest and broadest possible talent pool. That includes women (they make up half of the workforce), people of color, people with disabilities, Indigenous people, LGBTQ2+ people, newcomers, people from different religions (specifically "visible" religions), people with different political backgrounds, and, yes, straight, white, able-bodied men. Every group must be included, because talent can be found in each. Diversity is the means for tapping into the widest and broadest talent pool.

The secret of the creativity and innovation model is that it addresses "issues of injustice" without calling it that. It appeals to the motivations of those in power (often money) to affect change that will be long-lasting and impactful on society as a whole.

Key Takeaways

- There are two models of diversity and inclusion: the social justice model and the creativity and innovation model.

- Social justice focuses on addressing societal injustices.

- Creativity and innovation focuses on addressing challenges in society by leveraging the diversity of talent.

- Looking at D&I through a lens of creativity and innovation helps ensure that the change you're working toward is directly connected to the success of your organization, and that it ultimately will last!

THE BUSINESS CASE

A great many people loathe the idea of needing a business case for diversity and inclusion. Hasn't it been proven already?

A business case answers the "why" question: in this case, why is it important for an organization to focus on diversity and inclusion? Truthfully, proving the business case is an ongoing, daily activity. Recently, I delivered training to a large mining company, and I found myself in a disagreement about the importance of land acknowledgements for Indigenous Peoples. One person in the class felt that we shouldn't bother with them. Their argument was that Indigenous Peoples in North America were from somewhere else too. Although the latter point may perhaps be accurate (if you look at migration patterns from ten thousand-plus years ago, although that theory is hotly contested), I made the case about how important it is for descendants of colonists to acknowledge the past—something I believe very strongly in as part of my role in reconciliation. If the business case were proven, then that conversation wouldn't have occurred. If the case had already been made, everyone in the room would have understood that land acknowledgements are vital to the reconciliation process, and that in fact, reconciliation is incredibly important to the inclusion of Indigenous talent.

I'm a big believer in having a rock-solid business case when doing this work. It should be the bedrock on which employers build their diversity and inclusion strategy. Without a solid foundation, the chances of success are diminished. You can't build a house without a foundation. (That will likely be the only construction reference in this book.)

Without a business case—one that stands the test of time—you run the risk of losing ground when something changes unexpectedly. For example, the economic slowdown of 2008 revealed which employers had bought into the business case for D&I and which were on rocky footing. Some employers maintained and increased their D&I budgets because they recognized the importance of their D&I journey. Conversely, some employers, taking massive steps backward, slashed budgets and laid off D&I practitioners. If diversity and inclusion is a key business priority, as many employers say it is, then it deserves the same type of commitment as any other key priority.

Although some people may not resonate with the term "business case" because it tends to be very "private sector," my point is that your organization's business case should address *why* your organization should focus on diversity and inclusion. Whether you call it a business case or something else, it needs to explain the reasoning behind creating and executing a diversity and inclusion strategy. What you call it doesn't matter to me—as long as it works for you.

In the coming pages, I focus on three fundamental areas that will have the most impact on your business case: *People*, *Customers*, and *Brand*.

There are two other important areas—compliance and supplier diversity. I don't love compliance because I don't think employers should be forced to do something that is good for their business. And supplier diversity is a relatively advanced conversation. I include a bit of information about legislation so that you know in general terms what your legal obligations are, but I'm going to otherwise skip delving into compliance and supplier diversity and save them for another time.

People

"People" is probably the easiest area for an organization to focus on because it's directly within the control of an employer and can be done with relatively little investment of time and money. People is about who you attract, retain, and promote. People is also about engagement: how engaged your people are directly affects how productive they are, which directly impacts your profitability.

And I know I referred to "profit." I'm sorry to those within nonprofit and public sector organizations for using such an evil word. But let me loop you in on a little secret: all organizations function similarly. Money in and money out. You may not be focused on making a profit per se, but you can spend only as much money as you have coming in and/or have borrowed—hence, this equation works for you too. "Profitability" means stretching your budget so you can get more done with the little you have to work with.

Unless you're an independent, self-employed contractor with no staff or subcontractors, regardless of what industry you're in or what your organization does, you have people working for you. (At least until our robot overlords get tired of humanity and shoot us all into outer space via a giant cannon. I really need to stop binge-watching Netflix.) Who are your people? Do you know how your people identify? If not, you should consider conducting a self-identification census (see the topic of measurement, page 117). Even if you make an educated guess (which I don't encourage; you can't just stop and do a census right now—you have a book to read), ask yourself this: Are your people representative of your customer?

Mitigating factors will always influence the demographic representation of your potential talent pool. For example, from 2006 to 2016, at least 92 percent of nurses in Canada were women.[1] That isn't good or bad. It just is. Some professions tend to attract more of certain groups than others, for whatever reason. And yes, we could stop and discuss bias in the education system that gently shoves more women into professions like nursing, but that conversation is for another book.

What you should be aspiring to is an employee population that represents the available workforce population and/or the community that you serve. If there is incongruence in that representation, that's where you have to ask some questions:

Is the incongruence related to the available talent? In the case of nurses, as it relates to biological sex, there is an industry incongruence. Females far outnumber males in the profession. That's not something you can fix with a targeted recruiting campaign. It requires a prolonged effort by the entire industry. Hint, hint.

Is the incongruence something we can address? In the example of nursing, arguably the incongruence isn't something one employer could deal with on its own, certainly not in the short term. Although employers should encourage different groups into their specific professions (men into nursing, women into engineering, Indigenous people into law), that's the long game. That type of effort can take more than a decade to bear fruit and requires partnerships with educational institutions, government, and industry associations. Where there is an incongruence related to the representation of available talent, that is within your control. Keeping with our nursing example, if I worked for Emory Hospital in Atlanta, Georgia, and the majority of nurses were white, that's an incongruence that can be addressed based on the population of nurses in the greater Atlanta area. Since over 50 percent of Atlanta residents are African American, hiring from the available talent would mean that over 50 percent of nurses in that city were

African American. It is therefore statistically improbable for the majority of the nurses at that hospital to be white.

Is there relative representation in other areas? Keeping intersectionality in mind, and continuing with the example of nursing, even if the majority of nurses are women, employers should look to whether there is incongruence between their workforce and the diversity of personal characteristics, such as race and ability, in the available talent pool. Look at how well your workforce represents your specific community. For example, according to the 2016 Census, 78 percent of residents of the city of Markham, Ontario, identify as something other than Caucasian.[2] As a result, we would expect to see a nursing population similar to that representation, unless there are some mitigating circumstances. If the nursing population at hospitals in Markham is predominantly white (and I should note that I haven't checked to find out if it is), you would have to ask yourself a question: Why? Again, it's not bad or good. You just have to understand the reasons. If the incongruence is because of a barrier, you have the power to remove that barrier and thus change the demographics of your workforce so that it is in line with the community that you are serving.

By the Numbers

Whenever I make the case for D&I, I tend to turn to my friends in government (like Statistics Canada and the US

Census Bureau) for the numbers. Numbers never lie, even if you just want them to tell you you're pretty. You may not like them, but that doesn't mean they're not telling you the truth. And before you say, "Hey, 73.6 percent of all statistics are made up," that's not true.[3] Someone said it a few times and people started to believe it. That's an argument used by people who don't like the statistics.

The numbers (from *reliable* sources) paint a very clear picture of why any employer should be applying a specific effort to diversify its workforce and make sure the workplace is inclusive and accessible. I call it the demographics tsunami: a wall of change that is suddenly upon us even though we've known it was coming for decades.

Women

Statistics Canada reports that Canada has a working-age population of around 24,635,400 (people aged fifteen to sixty-five). Of those, just shy of half (49.8 percent) identify as female.[4] In the United States, 50.6 percent of the working-age population is female. So, from the start, you've got a 50/50 split on sex, which means employers need to make sure their workplaces are inclusive and examine their practices and policies so that females can rise to the top just as their male colleagues can.

Yes, there are mitigating circumstances. There are more women in nursing, more men in policing, *blah blah blah*. I'm not here to argue the circumstances. However, when we look at children and teens under the age of fifteen, 48.7 percent in Canada and 48.9 percent in the United States are female. At some point those little monsters are going to decide what they want to do when they grow up, besides being Internet famous. This is a perfect opportunity for employers to encourage said little darlings into "nontraditional" careers, such as by encouraging boys to look at nursing and girls to consider policing. Just a thought, but it won't happen if employers don't step up. The way society, education, and the media work, if we do nothing, we will continue to see the imbalance in certain professions.

However, take note: we can actually be born into three potential sexes—male, female, and intersex. According to the Intersex Society of North America (ISNA), intersex is "a general term used for a variety of conditions in which a person is born with a reproductive or sexual anatomy that doesn't seem to fit the typical definitions of female or male."[5] According to the ISNA, the instances of intersex births run between one in 1,500 and one in 2,000.[6] Not big numbers, but there is a percentage of people who have to lie on their census because they have the options of only "male" and "female."

On top of that, the census question is, "What is your sex?" Sex is assigned at birth. The doctor pulls the baby out, looks down at its junk, and makes a declaration: boy or girl (except in the instance of intersex babies, when they have to call in a specialist in sex differentiation). Arguably, the question of biological sex is irrelevant in the census (if not in every instance). The question should be, "What is your gender?"

and the options should be broad enough to include people who are gender nonbinary (not exclusively masculine or feminine) and gender nonconforming ... or, as my friend Kai likes to say, "gender fabulous." We have no idea how many people do not fit into the binary world of male and female.

Age

For the first time in history, we now potentially have five generations in the workforce. The generations are:

- Traditionalists or the silent generation: born before 1945
- Baby boomers: born between 1946 and 1964
- Generation X: born between 1965 and 1979
- Generation Y or millennials: born between 1980 and 1994
- Generation Z or the iGeneration: born after 1995.[7]

These generations have been given a raft of different names and dates, but suffice it to say this all means that the workforce ranges in age from fifteen to ninety-five. Although it's unlikely that most Traditionalists are still working, some do. How many Walmart greeters have you seen under the age of seventy? And while the youngest of iGen may not be working at the tender age of eight (unless they're on *Toddlers and Tiaras*), their twenty-four-year-old siblings likely are. It is entirely possible to have someone in their twenties managing a person in their seventies.

People of Color

According to the 2016 Census, 22.3 percent of Canadians identify as a "visible minority."[8] But in reviewing the data from the census and looking *solely* at the ethnic or cultural origin selected (not at whether a person identifies as a "visible minority"), I found that the percentage of respondents who are racialized people in Canada is 28.4 percent. In the United States, as of 2010, 40.5 percent of the population identified as people of color.

Regardless of the exact numbers, somewhere around 25 percent of Canadians and 40 percent of Americans have an ethno-cultural heritage that would be considered "racialized" or "of color." That number can swing dramatically up in places like Toronto and Atlanta (each over 50 percent) or significantly down in places like Moncton, New Brunswick, and Boise, Idaho (7.2 percent and 17.7 percent, respectively). These numbers are only going to increase, and employers need to ensure their workplaces are inclusive and free of racism so that they can tap into this labor market.

People with Disabilities

The percentage of working-age Canadians who report living with a disability of some kind is 13.7 percent, which works out to one in seven Canadians.[9] The numbers in the United States are slightly lower, at 10.6 percent, or one in ten Americans. Those numbers shift dramatically with age.

These numbers have grown in recent years for two primary reasons. First, we have an aging workforce, and the numbers indicate that the older people get, the more likely they are to develop a disability. Second, our understanding of disability has grown dramatically. We know much more about disability today than we did fifty years ago. The list of things considered "disabilities" according to law is quite extensive. According to the Canadian Disability Reference Guide:

> *Disability* is a complex phenomenon, reflecting an interaction between features of a person's body and mind and features of the society in which they live. A disability can occur at any time in a person's life; some people are born with a disability, while others develop a disability later in life. It can be permanent, temporary or episodic. Disability can steadily worsen, remain the same, or improve. It can be very mild to very severe. It can be the cause, as well as the result, of disease, illness, injury, or substance abuse.[10]

People with disabilities are a significant untapped talent pool. According to Statistics Canada, in 2012 the rate of unemployment among people with disabilities (of working age) was 11 percent, compared with 6 percent for the working-age population of Canadians who don't live with a disability.[11] The United States has similar splits, with 7.3 percent unemployment among people with disabilities compared with 3.5 percent of those not identifying as living with a disability.[12]

Indigenous Peoples

Indigenous Peoples, which includes First Nations, Inuit, and Métis people, make up 4.9 percent of the Canadian population.[13] Often referred to as Native Americans or American Indians in the United States, Indigenous people make up 1.3 percent of the population in that country. More importantly, Indigenous communities are growing significantly. In the United States, between 2000 and 2010, the Native American population grew by 26.7 percent, whereas the non-Indigenous population grew by 9.7 percent. In Canada, from 2006 to 2016, the population of Indigenous people grew 42.5 percent— more than four times the growth rate of the non-Indigenous population.

Not only is the Indigenous population growing quickly, it's also significantly younger. The average age of an Indigenous person in Canada is thirty-two, in comparison to a non-Indigenous person at forty-one. In the United States, the median age of the Native American population is twenty-nine, eight years younger than the median age of the non-Indigenous population.

The potential talent pool among Indigenous people is significant, but it requires employers to learn how to integrate Indigenous cultures with their own, in a way that is respectful and inclusive. It's not as simple as saying, "Let's hire Indigenous people." There is work to be done to ensure that the workplace is inclusive for Indigenous people.

Immigrants

North America is made up of immigrants. I identify as a British mutt (a little bit Irish, English, Welsh, and Scottish). My people have been in North America for more than two hundred years, but we still "come from away." I'm a proud Canadian. My blood flows maple-leaf-flag red. But I know where my people come from.

According to the 2016 Canadian Census, 21.9 percent of respondents identified that they had been, at some time, a landed immigrant or permanent resident.[14] That is only slightly lower than the all-time high of 22.3 percent, which was recorded in 1921. In 2016, the number of foreign-born respondents (not citizens) in the United States was 13.5 percent or 43,739,345, which, to keep things in perspective, is more than the entire population of Canada. (Enter feelings of inadequacy.) These numbers clearly show that now, more than ever, employers need to ensure they are creating inclusive workplaces for newcomers, while providing training on intercultural competence to ensure their workforce has the skills to manage people with different expectations about the workplace.

LGBTQ2+

We don't know how many LGBTQ2+ people there are in the world, let alone North America. Little data is available. Thanks to American biologist Alfred Kinsey, the LGBTQ2+ population was long believed to be 10 percent, but his study was done in 1948 and has pretty much been disproven. A poll conducted by Forum Research for the *National Post* found that 5 percent of Canadians identified as LGBTQ2+.[15] Gallup conducted a similar study that found 4.5 percent of Americans identified as LGBTQ2+.[16] That's obviously lower than Kinsey's findings, but it's the best we have so far. It is commonly accepted that the population is somewhere between 6 to 8 percent, which is not a small number.

Generally speaking, this is an invisible minority. Although not universally true, many LGBTQ2+ people can "pass" (as straight and/or cisgender), so their coworkers may not even know about their identity. A report from the Canadian Centre for Diversity and Inclusion (CCDI) found that 27.6 percent of sexual minorities (lesbian, gay, bisexual, queer, and other) are not "out" in the workplace, while 33.4 percent are out to everyone at work. Conversely, 39 percent of gender minorities (trans, gender nonbinary, and all gender minorities) are not out to anyone in the workplace, and only 13.6 percent are out to everyone.[17]

The research shows that the majority of LGBTQ2+ people limit how out they are at work for a variety of reasons, most frequently fear of reprisal and fear of their identity being a limiting factor in their career progression. The takeaway here is that if LGBTQ2+ people do not feel comfortable coming out at work, then their level of engagement will be negatively affected, which is ultimately bad for business.

Religious Minorities

New-ish to the diversity conversation are people of religious minorities. My mother always said the two things to keep out of work were politics and religion, but that isn't the case anymore, and I'm certainly not going to start listening to her now. Traditionally, one might think about people from more "visible" faiths, such as some Muslims, Hindus, and Sikhs, and some sects of Judaism. However, in recent years there has been an increase in nondominant religions and faiths bringing their whole self to work: Coptic and Eastern Orthodox Christians, Buddhists, Jains, Bahá'í, and Zoroastrians.

CCDI offers a service called a Diversity Meter, which allows employers to collect anonymous and confidential demographic data on their employees. Data collected for clients using CCDI's Diversity Meter service shows a decrease in people identifying as Christian (particularly younger people) but an increase in non-Christian faiths. It would be a mistake for employers to ignore this potential talent pool, and so they need to educate themselves on these differences, to make people from various faiths feel included. For example, could you consider rotating or flexible religious holidays? In the Western context, we have two statutory holidays that stem from Christianity. What if you offered flexible holidays that could be taken whenever it is appropriate for the individual? That would send a strong message to people who don't identify as Christian about how welcome they are in your workplace.

How Many SWAMs Are There?

Given all of the potential groups in the diversity conversation, I've often wondered how many SWAMs there actually are in the potential workforce. Considering their dominance in some professions and certainly in senior positions, I thought it would be interesting to look at the numbers and figure it out.

Warning: there is about to be math. According to Statistics Canada, as of the 2016 Census, Canada's entire population was 36,708,100, give or take, and you'll recall that the working-age population of people between fifteen and sixty-five totals 23,376,530.[18] Right away, we're talking about only 64 percent of Canadians. Numbers from the US Census Bureau indicate that 62 percent of Americans are of working age.[19] The table below shows the details, but here's how I arrived at the number of SWAMs in the workplace:

- I subtracted working-age women from the total working-age population.

- From the remainder, I subtracted the percent of working-age men who identify as a "visible minority" or person of color.

- From the remainder of that, I subtracted the percent of working-age men who identify as Indigenous or Native American.

- From the remainder of that, I subtracted the percent of working-age men who identify as living with a disability.

- From the remainder of that, I subtracted 5 percent to account for the portion of the white LGBTQ2+ population that identifies as male.

	CANADA		UNITED STATES	
Group	Number	Percent	Number	Percent
Working-age population	23,376,530	100.00%	206,686,217	100.00%
Working-age women	11,800,400	49.52%	107,170,000	48.15%
Working-age men of color	3,725,090	15.94%	44,475,550	21.52%
Working-age Indigenous and Native American men	813,520	3.48%	1,393,210	0.67%
Working-age men living with a disability*	884,843	3.79%	9,934,840	4.81%
Working-age LGBTQ2+ men**	618,445	2.65%	2,752,033	1.33%
Straight, white, able-bodied men	7,459,945	31.91%	42,353,793	20.49%

*Based on 2012 data
** This is an estimate

Although admittedly this is not 100 percent accurate (the data is a bit inconsistent in terms of quality, and I am not an actuary), it starts to paint a picture that around 30 percent of the Canadian workforce and 20 percent of the American workforce would identify as straight, white, able-bodied, and male. That number will swing significantly in places like Toronto and Atlanta, where it is below 10 percent, and up in places like Moncton and Boise, where it is closer to 50 percent.

Your workforce should look like the community that you serve, not necessarily like Canada or the United States overall. If you operate in Toronto or Atlanta, the percentage of your workforce that are people of color should be over 50 percent, but if you operate in Moncton or Boise, it should be significantly less than the national average.

All you need to take away from the "People" part of the D&I business case is that your workforce—your people—should look like the available talent and the community that you serve. And if it doesn't, you should start asking *why* it doesn't.

Why does it matter? It matters because if you're not thinking about the demographics of who you're hiring, you're potentially missing out on talent and not actually hiring the best and brightest. Let's look at an example within the legal profession. Recruiting in law is a relatively simple process. After students graduate from law school, they have to article (meaning work a certain number of hours) before they can qualify to be called to the Bar. (Personally, I've spent more than enough hours in a bar to qualify as something. Not the point.) Most law students article at law firms. There are other avenues to take, but the majority get their hours this way.

For at least twenty-five years, law schools have been about 50/50 women and men. In major cities like Toronto and New York, law schools tend to be ethnically balanced as well, about 50/50 between white and people of color. Now let's assume that a firm selects one hundred students to interview based on their grades and applications. And let's pretend for a moment that the one hundred students are 50 percent men and 50 percent women, and 50 percent white and 50 percent people of color. Because statistically they should be.

Then let's look at the photo of the students who were successfully hired at a certain firm in a large city (the name and location have been excluded to protect the guilty), where we see a group of twenty-five attractive young people, relatively balanced between men and women, yet all but one are white. If they interviewed one hundred students, and the firm hired one student from a group of fifty and twenty-four students from the other group of fifty, this is what is called *statistically improbable*. Not impossible, but highly unlikely.

It's a safe bet that the firm in question had bias in their hiring process and, simply put, didn't hire the best and brightest among the bunch. There are other variables, but it's safe to say they missed out on talent. You cannot say with any certainty that the twenty-five students they hired were the best and brightest. Some of them may be, but not all. It's just not possible. That's not opinion. It's math.

Your hiring should be reflective of the community because, if it is, statistically speaking, you should be hiring the best and brightest talent and not missing out.

Customers

Every organization has customers. You may not refer to them as such, and in fact you may recoil from the word "customer," but if we're being honest, it's all the same. Who do you do your work for? A hospital's customer is its patient; a municipality's customer is its resident or citizen; a hotel's customer is its guest. A concrete manufacturer's customer is... a person who buys concrete. Every organization has customers in some way, shape, or form, regardless of what you call them.

What it all comes down to is this: Do you understand the needs of your customer? Who are your customers? What do they look like? What matters to them? To serve your customer properly, you must understand your customer's needs. If you want to do business with China, you had best understand their cultural norms, lest you end up with egg foo yung on your face (see what I did there?).

Even at home, it's important that you understand the needs of your customers. There's a well-known story among D&I practitioners (which may or may not be true, but let's just go with it) that tells of a chief marketing officer (CMO) of one of the big Canadian banks. The bank had made it a priority to market into Canada's South Asian community. The bank was being pitched by an advertising agency, and when said CMO met with the agency, he didn't even let them do their pitch. Immediately after the introductions, he told the agency team that when they looked more like his prospective customers, he'd come back. Until then, he wasn't interested in what they had to say, and he left the meeting. There's a similar story floating around about Beyoncé Knowles and Reebok, but Reebok denies it.[20] Whether or not these stories are true, they articulate the importance of understanding your customers. And how do you get to understand your customers? By reflecting them.

Let me be perfectly clear: that doesn't mean you should have "tokens." I can't tell you the number of meetings I've heard about where the black/East Asian/woman administrative assistant was taken to a client pitch to show the organization's commitment to diversity. That's just rude and quite stupid, to be blunt. If the client really cares about the diversity of your team, don't you think they'll ask the assistant questions that person won't be equipped to answer? I'm shaking my head just thinking about it.

D&I is not about tokenism. Please don't hire people because of their sex or the color of their skin. Think about diversity and inclusion as part of your hiring process to ensure that your team represents your clients and your community. The people you hire need to be able to do the job. And before you say, "We can't find them"—they're not hiding! You're just not looking hard enough, or your hiring process isn't truly fair and equitable. Check out chapter 6, "Attracting Difference," for more on talent attraction (page 89).

Brand

When I speak of "brand," I'm talking about the entire public impression of your organization. Your brand is so much more than your logo, and it directly impacts your people and your customer.

How is your brand perceived in the market? Do people think of it and say, "That's a place I want to work," because it's diverse and inclusive? Or do people think, "I don't believe I'll be welcome there"? Your brand can include many things:

- The images you use on your website and in marketing materials. Are they representative of your people and your customer?

- The language you use on your website and in marketing materials. Do you say things like "X is an equal-opportunity employer" or "X aspires to have a workforce that is representative of the diversity of our country and encourages applications from everyone"? One of those is great language. The other is not. I'll let you guess which is which. (Ahem, it's the second one.)

- The languages in which you advertise. Almost 23 percent of Canadians have a nonofficial mother tongue, and 69.9 percent of those speak their mother tongue at home. In the United States, 13.4 percent of the population speak Spanish at home.[21]

- Participation in events that specifically target potential communities, whether as talent or customer. Do you participate in festivals (such as those celebrating LGBTQ2+ pride, Diwali, Lunar New Year, Cinco de Mayo, and so on)? Do you engage with community groups? Do you sponsor events? All those activities send a message about your priorities.

That list is just scratching the surface of the potential impact of D&I on your brand. Apply a D&I lens to your brand to attract the broadest range of talent and customers.

The Research

I could fill a room with research that shows the positive impact diversity and inclusion can have on both the top and bottom line of an organization. Truthfully, there's *no* research (or at least none that I've been able to find) that proves the potential negative influence of embracing diversity and inclusion. There is opinion, but *opinion is not research*. Just because you think it's true doesn't actually make it true. The only qualifier I will add is that I'm talking about employers who *do D&I right*.

If you Google "negative effects of diversity in the workplace," you will uncover some materials that suggest potential outcomes. One article clearly outlines six potential negative impacts: communication issues, lack of freedom of speech, increased cost of training, integration issues, increased competition, and disrespect.[22] With all due respect to the author (whose name is conspicuously missing from the article), they're wrong. I could argue every point the author made quite easily, but each would come back to one thing: diversity needs to be done right! Besides, this is an article—not genuine research. Opinion and fact are not the same thing.

But there are two pieces of research that I will point to that clearly support the business case for D&I.

Waiter, Is That Inclusion in My Soup?

The 2013 report "Waiter, Is That Inclusion in My Soup: A New Recipe to Improve Business Performance," by Deloitte Australia and the Victorian Equal Opportunity and Human Rights Commission, does a wonderful job of showing the positive impact that D&I can have on an organization.[23] Without giving away the ending (Rosebud is a sled), they surveyed 1,550 people and found that diversity and inclusion can play a significant role in the engagement of employees. In short, organizations with a significant focus on diversity, and whose employees feel included, saw a lift on engagement scores of as much as 101 percent in comparison with organizations that had little to no commitment to diversity and whose employee population didn't feel included.

This study offers many insights, and it is but one that shows the direct impact D&I can have on engagement, which ultimately leads to higher levels of productivity and profitability.

Diversity Matters and Delivering through Diversity

McKinsey and Company's 2015 report "Diversity Matters" examined proprietary data for 366 public companies across a range of industries in Canada, Latin America, the United Kingdom, and the United States.[24] Specifically, they looked at the financial performance of those 366 companies and the demographic makeup of the senior management and boards of directors. The report reveals two key findings:

- Companies in the top quartile for racial and ethnic diversity are 35 percent more likely to have financial returns above their respective national industry medians.

- Companies in the top quartile for gender diversity are 15 percent more likely to have financial returns above their respective national industry medians.[25]

McKinsey followed up this report with further research released in early 2018, called "Delivering through Diversity."[26] The more recent report further shows the correlation between diversity and inclusion and the financial performance of an organization.

Fact and Choice

Here's another catchy quip for the mix: Diversity is a fact. Inclusion is a choice. (And that one you can attribute to me.)

Diversity is a fact. When two human beings are in one place, you have diversity of some kind. It may not be obvious, but it is diversity all the same. No one has a lived experience identical to anyone else—not even identical twins, because their lived experiences will necessarily have diverged, even a little. We're all unique snowflakes. (Can I put the barf emoji here?)

Diversity is around you all the time—and has been since the dawn of civilization— whether you like it or not! You don't have to like it, but disliking it won't make it go away. As my uncle-in-law says, "You can wish in one hand and poop in the other and see which one fills up first." (He uses other language, but I'll be polite.) What does influence whether or not you achieve diversity in your organization are your efforts to welcome it. And that's where inclusion comes in.

Inclusion is a choice. Nothing says you *must* be inclusive. Yes, we have laws that protect people from discrimination based on certain traits, but there's always a way around them. In 2013, the Ontario Human Rights Commission (OHRC) issued a policy statement that said there *may* be grounds for a human rights complaint if a person were refused a job because of a lack of "Canadian experience."[27] Believe it or not, newcomers to Canada, regardless of their country of origin, constantly hear that excuse to explain why they're not right for a job.

Take the example of my husband. I married an American and he moved to Canada to be with me. When Mike (yes, we're in a same-name relationship) moved to Canada, he applied for numerous jobs. At the time, he had twenty-one years of experience in accounting with some of the world's largest corporations. Yet we lost count of how many times he was told he didn't have any "Canadian experience." My American, English-as-a-first-language, white, able-bodied husband was told that somehow his twenty-one years of experience weren't as valuable as a person with less—albeit Canadian—experience, because math is somehow different in Canada than it is in the United States!

Do you think anything changed for newcomers when the OHRC issued its policy statement? Absolutely not. The excuses just changed. Employers chose *not* to be inclusive.

But employers that *choose* to create inclusive cultures benefit. Whether including internationally trained professionals, women, racialized people, or any other group that is in the "minority," inclusion is a choice that can have a significantly positive impact on the top and bottom line of an organization, through longer tenure and lower rates of voluntary turnover, lower rates of absenteeism and presenteeism, lower safety incidents, and on and on. Being inclusive can save you money!

At the end of the day, when you look at the data, the business case is provable. It needs to speak the language of your organization; it needs to include data that is relevant to your organization; and it needs to make the case that diversity and inclusion is a business priority, not a "nice to have." For some assistance on developing a business case, take a look at CCDI's *Toolkit: Locking in Your Leadership: Developing the Ironclad Business Case for D&I*.[28] It's a great free resource to get you started. You can find it here: https://ccdi.ca/toolkits/.

A Word on Legislation

I would be remiss if I didn't include a section that covers legislation that influences an employer's diversity and inclusion work. There are multiple legislations that may have an impact. The unfortunate part of including a section like this is that it gets frozen in amber. The moment after we print the book, legislation will change. There are an endless number of potential legislations, depending on your city, state, or province, not to mention the country you're in.

The headline here is that compliance with legislation is *not diversity and inclusion work*. It's compliance. Legislation is rarely "leading practice." It establishes a minimum standard. Truly progressive organizations go well above and beyond the requirements of the law.

Once upon a time I worked for an employer (that shall remain nameless) that was subject to the Employment Equity Act. When I started in my role, I went to the head of HR and raised the red flag that the organization was not in compliance with the act, which could impact revenue significantly, as there are big fines for noncompliance. The response I got: "Are we going to get caught?"

Legislation is not optional. You should not aspire to do the minimum with these laws. You should take the intention of the law and go above it.

All that said, even though I'm not going to spend a ton of ink on legislation, on CCDI's site I have summarized some of the potential legislations you might be dealing with (see michaelbach.com/legislation), but by no means is the list definitive. The best thing you can do is know what laws you are subject to and what you have to do to comply with them.

Key Takeaways

- Your business case (or whatever you choose to call it) addresses why your organization needs to focus on diversity and inclusion.

- Your business case should focus on three areas: people, customers, and brand.

- Make sure your business case speaks the language of your organization, and simply and succinctly proves the case for D&I.

- Know the legislation in your city, province, state, and country, and—at a minimum—comply with it.

THE RIGHT WAY
TO DO DIVERSITY

This is the question I don't get asked enough: "How do you 'do' diversity and inclusion *right*?" If more employers asked that question, we'd be a lot further along and not facing down the demographic tsunami that looms above our heads. In some senses, there isn't a right or wrong way to do diversity. But then again, I'm a man of many contradictions, so allow me to contradict myself.

You certainly can do D&I the wrong way if you think that it will happen on its own, just because you believe it will; if you believe your organization is a meritocracy where everyone is treated equally, but you've never actually examined whether that's true; if you don't apply an appropriate budget and resources to focus on changing your culture; and so on. The list of potential "wrongs" is far longer than the list of "rights."

Beyond organizations that solely focus on compliance, let me give you an example of diversity done wrong. A certain American company wanted to capture some of the LatinX/ Hispanic market, which is worth billions of dollars (LatinX is a gender-neutral alternative to "Latina" or "Latino"). Said company decided they were going to get a piece of the action. They planned to open stores in predominantly Hispanic communities. They created advertisements and marketing campaigns in Spanish. They poured a lot of money into positioning themselves as attractive for the LatinX/Hispanic communities. And then, on day one, they opened their doors and ... not a single person behind the counter spoke Spanish. None of the documentation was in Spanish. All in all, it was a total disaster. The community started asking questions, like "How many LatinX/Hispanic executives do you have?" and "Do you have a LatinX/Hispanic employee resource group?" and "How much are you spending to support the LatinX/ Hispanic communities through sponsorship of community organizations?" Not a good day for the employee who was responsible for the launch. Sorry ... *former* employee.

It's easy to do diversity wrong. In this case, a bunch of white people tried to design an offering without any input from the potential customer.

If there's a wrong way, there's a right way, right? Sort of. There is a road map—a compass of sorts—that can help you navigate this deep and complicated topic. In this chapter, I'll outline the steps that every organization should follow if they want to be on the right track with their diversity and inclusion journey.

The Road Map for Diversity and Inclusion

Before you read further, know that you can't skip a single step in the following process, so please don't try to. You don't have to start at the beginning if you've been on a diversity and inclusion journey for some time, but if you think you're at step 3 and you never did step 1, guess where you need to start? The steps are in a particular order for a reason—to build something from the ground up. Remember, the house needs a good foundation.

Step 1: Your Business Case

This is the step that gets skipped the most. Some people think we're past the business case because we have so much data to prove the case, and in a lot of ways we are, but just because *you* understand the business case doesn't mean *everyone* understands the business case.

A diversity and inclusion business case is a two- to three-page document that answers "why" questions. Why is your organization focused on diversity and inclusion? Why does it matter? Why do you need a D&I focus to make you more competitive in your market? Why do you want to better serve your community? Why does your brand rely on attracting top talent? You need to determine what the business case for your organization should include, specifically—but if you read the previous chapter, you know that it should focus on people, customer, and brand. You did read the last chapter, right? The intent of a business case is to educate decision makers and convince them to take action. In the case of D&I, I would argue that the "decision maker" is every person in your organization, and even people external to your organization.

You must be able to explain why D&I matters. This is a *critical* first step, and I can't overemphasize its importance. Some people reading this book may think, "I know why it matters"—but not everyone is convinced. If everyone had bought into the business case for diversity and inclusion, then the leadership of our organizations would look different. If everyone had bought in, we wouldn't see the onslaught of "isms" that we do in society. It's obvious that not everyone has bought in.

I've heard this a lot from clients: "We need to increase the diversity of our leadership." My response: Why? What's the demographic makeup of your leadership now? What does the pipeline look like? What are you doing to support and develop potential leaders? If I'm asking why, others will ask why, and you need to be able to answer that question clearly and concisely to convince whoever is asking.

Thinking things like "I know why it matters" tells me that you've engaged your heart but not necessarily your head. That type of thinking keeps us in the "it's the right thing to do" social justice model of D&I. Although important, it's not enough to ensure sustainable change. You have to engage your head. Engaging your head is about focusing on facts and data, which should be at the core of your business case.

People have power. *All* people have power. In some way, shape, or form, regardless of their level within your organization, people have the ability to undermine what you're aspiring to. If they don't see the importance of the work, they can subtly and quietly subvert it. That's where your business case comes in. It's the document that you start with and reference on a regular basis to remind you why you're doing the work you're doing. Personally, I like to think of a business case as my touchstone. It's the document I turn to regularly to remind me of why it matters.

Don't get me wrong: you can't simply turn to the naysayers and say, "Read this," and expect their minds to be completely changed. Far from it. However, you need to do the work up front by ensuring you have a rock-solid business case, so when said naysayers surface, you're able to respond to their objections coherently and unwaveringly. The keys to a good business case are:

KISS: keep it short and simple. Thanks to living in a world where we count characters rather than words, people have the attention span of goldfish. If you can't grab someone's attention in a page or two, you're not going to be successful with your hundred-page opus. Yes, I'm sure every word is brilliant... but it's not. Keep it short, simple, and to the point.

Make it organization-specific. Just because it works for one organization doesn't mean it will work for your organization. Your business case must speak the language of your organization. Do you even use the term "business case"? If not, what would be more appropriate? It's important that the document be consistent with everything else in your organization.

There are many resources available for writing a business case. CCDI put together a valuable resource called *Locking in Your Leadership: Developing the Ironclad Business Case for D&I*.[1] This is a guide to help people write a business case specific to diversity and inclusion. You can find it at https://ccdi.ca/toolkits/.

Step 2: Current-State Assessment

This is another step that gets skipped, but it is arguably even more important than step 1. If you don't know where you are, how do you know where you're going?

The purpose of the current-state assessment is to provide clarity around where you are today so that you can understand where you need to be tomorrow. In essence, it answers the "what" question. It's meant to provide a clear picture of what the issues are so that you can develop a strategy to address them. Otherwise, your strategy will be based on assumption, not fact.

Assessments such as these go by any number of names (Diversity Audit, Equity Assessment, Employment Systems Review), but at CCDI we call it a Current State Inclusivity Assessment (catchy yet obvious). We have our own methodology, but in general, assessments can include a variety of components:

A leadership assessment. What do your leaders think about diversity and inclusion? The tone from the top is one of the most critical pieces of a successful diversity and inclusion initiative. It's important to assess the leadership to understand how they feel about the topic and how they perceive the inclusivity of your organization.

Demographics. Who are your people? If you don't know who your people are, you won't know who you're missing out on.

An inclusion survey. How do your people feel about working for you? This isn't an engagement survey. An inclusion survey is a different beast. And remember—you *must* look at your inclusion survey through the lens of demographics, or you're missing the real story. It can also include things like focus groups and one-on-one interviews.

Maturity analysis. This piece of an assessment looks at how your organization is doing from a policy and procedure perspective. Do you have the right foundation to build on? The best way to assess your maturity, in my opinion, is to compare yourself to the Global Diversity and Inclusion Benchmarks (GDIB) from the Centre for Global Inclusion. The GDIB is a benchmarking tool that has been vetted by more than one hundred D&I specialists from around the world and is the soundest guide for self-assessment there is.

Competitor analysis. Looking at your competitors can be quite motivating. This part of the assessment looks at what is publicly available, and sometimes it involves the tried-and-true "pick up the phone and ask" method. Not every employer is motivated by this piece, but it can't hurt to understand what your competitors are doing in the D&I space. This information may help inspire your organization to focus on a particular area that may hold a gap in your plan.

Once you've gathered substantial information, you can conduct an analysis of it and produce a report that describes your current state, which also tells you where you might have opportunities. Although you could hire someone to do this for you, you can do it yourself, and it doesn't have to be a huge undertaking. For example, if you're not ready for a demographic census, consider what data you already have. Most labor codes require you to collect, at a minimum, data related to age and sex. While this doesn't provide the complete picture, at least it's something. Just be sure that you have done your due diligence around privacy laws so you know you can use the data for this purpose. While it's not the perfect solution, doing an assessment yourself is just about the legwork.

Step 3: Strategy

Now that you've done your assessment, you can develop your strategy. Your strategy answers the "how" question, and it is tactical. You know where the issues are, so you have to determine how you're going to address them. The shape of the strategy is completely up to you, but a few words of advice:

Speak your language. Your strategy needs to speak the language of the organization. In its presentation, it needs to look like it's part of everything you do. It needs to be something that makes anyone in the company think, "This is from where I work." Copying and pasting someone else's strategy won't work.

Be SMART. Make sure you use the SMART theory (Specific, Measurable, Actionable, Realistic, Timely) when coming up with your tactics.

Don't boil the ocean. It's typical for organizations, particularly when they're new to the diversity world, to try and do too much too fast. You may have a lot of issues to address, and your instinct may be to try to fix them all as quickly as possible. Don't do that. If you try to do twenty things in one year, you'll fail at all of them. Pick a few things and do them well. You might also want to size your action items as small, medium, and large. Then you can do a few small things, a couple of medium things, and one large thing. For example, a small action might be starting to celebrate different cultural and religious holidays. That's an easy win. A large action might be creating a sponsorship program for women in leadership.

CCDI developed a toolkit called *Locking in Your Leadership: Toolkit for Developing a Diversity and Inclusion Strategy*, which is available to download for free at https://ccdi.ca/toolkits/.

Step 4: Execute

Now that you have your business case, your assessment, and your strategy, you're ready to go! You just need to do the work. The "work" is transforming your strategy from paper into practice. This requires the biggest effort. You have to execute on the tactical actions in your strategy.

Step 5: Measurement

Measurement is another critical step that often gets forgotten. How do you know if you've been successful? You have to measure. What you measure is up to you, but you should include it as part of your strategy. For example, if you decide you need to increase the number of women in line for a leadership position, part of that work is about getting more women into the pipeline, and another part is constantly measuring the demographics of your pipeline. Otherwise, how do you know if you've been successful?

Measurement is so important that I dedicated all of chapter 8 to it. That starts on page 117.

Step 6: Rinse and Repeat

The beauty and torture of this work is that it doesn't end. You don't simply go through this process once and then you're all done. At specific intervals (such as yearly), you have to measure your success; but at some point (like every three to five years), you have to go back to the beginning and start over.

Not because you did anything wrong, but simply because you have to reassess to know if you're still on the right path. Repeating the process includes:

Reviewing the business case. It's a good idea to review your business case every once in a while to make sure it still applies. If you've written a good business case, you shouldn't have to make changes often. Update it as needed to address changing circumstances.

A current-state assessment. Repeat the assessment process described above, in step 2, to know if you're making progress or if other issues have come up.

Strategy. Develop a strategy to address the new or remaining issues.

Measurement. Measure, measure, measure. Enough said.

The Secret Ingredient

I often get asked what skills are required to be a good D&I practitioner, and if there's one thing I can stress, it's change management—or, as the *Oxford Dictionary* defines it, "the management of change and development within a business or similar organization."[2] In short, and quite obviously, it's about managing change. This isn't the most creative definition, but you get the point.

It's critically important to understand that diversity and inclusion work *is* change management work. It's about leading your organization through change. It can be small or large. But it is change. And news flash: nobody likes change. Even if people say they like change, they're lying. It's physiology: our brains don't like change. Change requires us to access parts of our brain that are normally not engaged. We have to think.

I came across a great article about real estate that sums it up well: "Everyone Loves Progress—Nobody Likes Change."[3] The same message applies to diversity and inclusion. This is especially true when the change is forced upon us, as has been the case in the economy in general, and in the real estate industry in particular. The result is that everyone—from the general public to industry leaders to the people we work with— is navigating unfamiliar waters. We don't know what's around the next corner, and so we're fearful and unsure.

The good news is that you can do a lot to calm frayed nerves and help others (and yourself) stay positive and productive. There are several models of change management out there—ADKAR, the McKinsey 7-S model, Nudge theory, the Kübler-Ross Change Curve—but whichever one you use, the bottom line is the same: change is hard, and it won't happen on its own. That's why change management is such a critical lens to apply to your diversity and inclusion work. As you're building your strategy, you have to apply a change management model to ensure that you're successful in your efforts.

When considering potential audiences (internal audiences, such as senior leadership, middle managers, and so on; or external, such as community groups, clients, partners), my personal favorite model of change management is the Five Fs, illustrated below.

| Fighters | Foes | Fence-Sitters | Friends | Family |

This model was taught to me by someone long ago, and I've never been able to find the source, but it still makes the most sense to me. It helps you understand where the issues may present themselves, and it suggests whom you will be able to influence more easily than others. Each category breaks down as follows:

- *Fighters* are committed to fighting the change. They are the active opposition.

- *Foes* are against the change, but they're a more passive opposition.

- *Fence-sitters* are exactly as they sound—neutral. They don't really care either way. They're not helping the change, but they're also not against it.

- *Friends* see the change as important but not critical. They are passively supportive.

- *Family* is committed to making the change work. They are your active supporters.

It's important to think of each audience, and in fact each individual, and where they might be on the continuum. Then you need to plan for them. How are you going to address the fears and resistance of your fighters? How are you going to address the apathy of your fence-sitters and turn them into friends? How are you going to engage your friends and get them active in the change? How are you going to ensure your family members don't let their passion get away from them and hinder your change? I like modeling this out and developing characters for each. For example, "Sally (a foe) is a middle manager who objects to the company's focus on diversity and inclusion." Build a profile for each group and figure out how you're going to engage with them.

Applying a change management approach to your diversity and inclusion strategy is imperative to ensure that the change lasts. If you follow these steps, the likelihood of your success increases significantly. It's not rocket science, but the difference between doing diversity right instead of wrong is all about process.

Key Takeaways

- Follow the six steps: make a business case, assess, strategize, execute, measure, repeat.

- To ensure successful change, it's imperative to follow the steps in order.

- Change management needs to be considered throughout.

INCLUSION OVER DIVERSITY (AKA TALENT RETENTION)

If you read the Contents page, you'll have seen that the chapter on talent retention comes before the chapter on talent attraction. This isn't a mistake. Although I wrote most of this book while drinking white wine (anything but chardonnay—it's not the '80s), I intentionally placed talent retention first because, simply put, it's more important. You heard me. Don't pretend like you didn't hear me.

I get asked a lot about which is more important—the diversity or the inclusion. Ultimately, the inclusion is more important than the diversity. If you don't have the inclusion, you won't have the diversity.

Let's make it biblical: if you hired a bunch of lambs, but until that point you had been hiring only lions, how do you think that's going to turn out? (To be clear, that may not be an actual biblical reference, but it feels like it might be.)

Many employers start out on their diversity and inclusion journey focusing on talent attraction and recruiting from different communities. This approach is what I like to call "wrong." As I mentioned, it's possible to attract a group through the front door only to find twice as many of that same group leaving out the back. One client I worked with had specifically developed a (very expensive) program to attract people of color to the organization, and it was going incredibly well. Until the company's voluntary turnover rates spiked. When we dug into the data, we saw that people of color were leaving at significantly higher rates than white people. So, we turned our focus to the culture and spent a significant amount of time on improving the workplace so that the diversity would stay. We made sure people were educated so they understood the individual's role in creating an inclusive culture. We reviewed policies and procedures to see if there were any unintentional biases at play. We looked at the unwritten rules (like how celebrations were always in the evening and always involved alcohol) and made changes to ensure our behavior wasn't inadvertently excluding people. We worked to make the culture inclusive.

If you're new to this journey (and even if you're not), you have to ensure your culture is open and welcoming to the diversity that you're trying to attract. As part of your assessment (see chapter 4, "The Right Way to Do Diversity," starting on page 67), you need to determine if your workplace is one where diversity will thrive, survive, or not remain alive. (Rhyming is fun.) Assuming you've done your assessment (you have, haven't you?), you'll have a sense of what the specific issues are to your organization. That said, generally speaking, there are some things you can do to create a more inclusive culture and retain talent.

Educate

Whether you're brand-new to diversity and inclusion or have been on the journey for decades, education is a critical component to your work. It isn't a "one and done" situation. New people join your organization every year. They come with their own perceptions and biases, and they could undermine everything you're trying to do. So, what do you need to keep in mind?

Have a learning map. From the day a person starts, there should be mandatory D&I training driven by a D&I learning map that takes each person through a learning journey, from the fundamentals (what diversity and inclusion means and why it is important in your organization) to more complex topics like unconscious bias and intercultural competence. You might also want to develop an assessment tool to customize the learning map for each person. Everyone joining your organization will have a different level of experience with diversity and inclusion. Don't force people to go through the D&I fundamentals when they've already had years of D&I training. An assessment tool ensures that each person gets relevant learning.

Learning doesn't have to be long. When people hear "learning," they usually think, "I'm going to have to pay people to take time off work to attend this." Yes and no. Although a half-day with Michael Bach is *super*-fun (and it really is), it's not necessarily practical to put all your people through that form of training. A series of short eLearning courses can have a similar (not *the same*) outcome, are far more cost-effective and sustainable, and are easier to roll out to your entire organization.

Learning is everywhere. Structured learning is one thing, but unstructured learning is equally as valuable. At the beginning of every team meeting, have a "diversity moment," when someone shares something about themselves to help educate their coworkers on the diversity that exists around them.

Focus on Leaders

I've said it before, and I'll say it again: tone from the top is critical. If your leaders don't understand the value of diversity and inclusion, you won't get anywhere. You need them to not only buy in, but also take ownership of the journey.

More often than not, a leader's perceptions of the organization are not in line with the employees' lived experiences. Leaders tend to not be fully aware of what's going on, particularly if they aren't members of an underrepresented group. I've seen situations in which leaders think the organization is perfect—there's no sexism, racism, homophobia, and so on. And then the employees' feedback reveals a dramatically different reality. The bigger the organization, the less likely its leaders will be attuned to the day-to-day, lived experience of its people.

Leaders need as much education as anyone else. Their learning programs should cover all the same information you push out to the rest of the organization, but they should also focus on a leader's role in creating an inclusive workplace. Their learning should be delivered in a safe space where they can be vulnerable and not feel like their staff will look at them differently. Or, as I like to say it, a place where they can safely stick their foot in their mouth. This could be in-person learning, eLearning, reading, or one-on-one assessments and coaching.

Communicate

Communication is the second most important key to the success of a D&I strategy (second only to leadership buy-in). You must communicate with your people about your diversity and inclusion work in a clear manner, and often. Why does it matter? How is it going to impact the daily lives of your people? What's in it for them? In the absence of information, people will fill in the blanks, and that is *not* something you want.

First, it's important to communicate your business case—to answer the "why" question before it's asked. Make sure that all your people understand why diversity and inclusion is vital to the success of your organization, and ensure that part of your communication answers WIIFM (what's in it for me?), so that individuals understand the positive impact your D&I strategy will have for them.

You also need to communicate the processes. When you start your assessment, communicate about what that process will look like. What's involved? What will you do with the information once you're done? Then, communicate about the results of the assessment. You don't have to post the entire report, but you should certainly share the highlights. The worst thing you can do is ask people in the organization to trust you and then stick your head in the sand. I saw this happen at one organization, and it had devastating effects on the organizational culture.

And you need to *keep* communicating, all throughout your journey (yes, that one that never ends). Communicate about celebrations, like Diwali and International Women's Day; about successes, such as when you hit a target or deliver a program; and even communicate about failures, like when you miss a target. (And you will, because you'll likely set unrealistic targets the first time out. Don't feel bad; it happens to everyone.) Being open and honest in your communication will engender a sense of respect and pride.

Communication is also a great way to educate, so ensure that you connect these strategies. You can't overcommunicate about D&I.

Re-examine Policies, Processes, and Procedures

How do things get done? For example, do you have an accommodation policy, and what does it accommodate? What's your recruiting process? What's your talent development procedure? What is the "written rule" of how something happens, and what is the "unwritten rule"?

Looking at all of your policies, processes, and procedures is a big piece of work and can be a very revealing one. For example, if you have a "maternity leave policy," it relates only to biological mothers, which excludes a lot of people—biological fathers, same-sex parents, adoptive parents, foster parents, and parents that use surrogates. A willingness to re-examine how things get done is critical. If you ever hear yourself say, "That's the way we've always done it," it's time to look under the hood. Just because you've always done it that way doesn't make it the right or best way.

These are just a few "broad brush" ideas of areas to focus on, but understand this: you need to customize your initiatives to suit your organization. Tailor your actions based on your assessment. If you don't, you may find yourself with a solution looking for a problem.

Key Takeaways

- Inclusion comes before diversity. You have to know that your culture is inclusive before you deliberately hire different people.

- Education is critical, and it can take a variety of forms.

- Communicate, communicate, communicate to ensure your entire organization buys into the D&I journey.

ATTRACTING DIFFERENCE

Once you've done your assessment and addressed any internal inclusion issues specific to your organization, it's time to develop initiatives that will attract difference. As I've explained, everyone is diverse. But you're looking for talent that is different from your current workforce. Hence, attracting *difference*.

I'll let you in on a little secret: you already have "diverse" people applying for jobs with your organization. They're not hiding. Unless you have an awful reputation as an employer, all types of people are applying. They're just not getting through the process. The first step in attracting different talent is to examine your talent-attraction process, and specifically to evaluate whether it includes barriers. The standard recruiting progression looks something like the steps that follow.

Job posting is created. Consider whether the language in your posting is inclusive. Are you using verbiage that is more appealing to one group over another? Do you think that's impossible? Think again. Carefully consider the language you use, and make sure it's not unintentionally sending the wrong message. For example, do you ever include stipulations such as "must be a good communicator" or, worse, "must be able to communicate well in English"? Communication is a completely subjective skill, and one person's understanding of "good communication" may be completely different from another's. If a potential applicant has English as a second-plus language, they may not apply because they don't think they're a good *enough* communicator in English, yet they may speak better English than some native speakers do. Instead of using language that encourages candidates to self-select out, devise a means to test all applicants' communication skills, if that's really a required skill.

Job posting is posted. Look at where you share your job posting. Do you post it on your website? On a job board like Indeed, Monster, or Workopolis? Doing that means you're fishing in the same barrel as everyone else. Have you ever considered posting your job on iHispano, Black Jobs, or Career Contessa? You have to go where the people are, not just where it's easiest for you to post. More on this below.

Candidates apply and are screened. Candidates are screened, either by an individual or by an applicant tracking system

(ATS) and then in person. This process is rife with potential issues. First, human beings have bias. If they're aware of their biases (for instance, they don't like immigrants, people with disabilities, LGBTQ2+ people, or women), they can deliberately screen out candidates who they *think* are from a certain group based on what they see in the application. If they're not aware of their biases, then they may be excluding candidates unconsciously.

Applicant tracking systems are also notoriously problematic. They use algorithms to screen candidates in and out. But algorithms are built by people, and people have biases, as Amazon found out in 2018. They had to scrap an AI-driven talent-attraction process because they discovered that their AI didn't like women. Quoting from the article from Reuters: "In effect, Amazon's system taught itself that male candidates were preferable. It penalized résumés that included the word 'women', as in 'women's chess club captain.' And it downgraded graduates of two all-women's colleges, according to people familiar with the matter. They did not specify the names of the schools."[1]

The problem with the first sentence in that quote is that it suggests the system learned it on its own. Bias is a taught behavior, even to computers. An ATS is not a foolproof way to sort talent, but it's the best we have so far, particularly when you might get a thousand applicants for a job, nine hundred of which aren't qualified. The question is: What screening requirements have we (the flawed humans) included?

Candidates are interviewed. Next comes evaluating your interviewing process. Sometimes this starts with a phone screening, and sometimes with the in-person portion of the program. Either way, interviews are often rife with potential problem areas where candidates could be screened out. Here's a short list of questions you might ask about your organization's process:

- Do you use standard questions for all candidates? You should, so that you ensure everyone is judged on the same criteria.

- Do you use structural or behavior questions, or a combination? I prefer a combination, which allows for variety, but it also depends on the role you're hiring for.

- Do you provide questions to candidates in advance? Although this is not a requirement, it certainly helps candidates prepare, particularly since interviewing can be quite stressful.

- Do you ask candidates about any accommodations they might require? This is D&I 101, and you should ask about and provide an accommodation to anyone who requests one.

- Are your facilities barrier-free? If they're not, this could be a significant issue for a person with mobility issues, which is why asking about accommodation is important.

- Are all your recruiters and hiring managers trained on bias in the hiring process? They should be.

- Do you interview one-on-one or in panels? A panel interview ensures that every person who is part of the process hears the same answers at the same time, and thus it helps to reduce the opportunity for bias.

- Do you use a scoring rubric? How do you know if an answer is good or bad? If you do use a rubric, do you judge the candidate based on an aggregate score? Again, you should.

That's the list I came up with in the short space of time that I spent waiting for a server to pour me a glass of pinot. There are so many potential areas of opportunity where employers can lose out on talent, not because the candidates don't have the skills and experience you're looking for, but because of the biases and barriers that exist in the process.

Candidate is hired. Once you've narrowed things down to the candidate of your choosing, you enter the negotiation. The problem: not everyone knows how to negotiate. In some cultures, there is no negotiation, or asking for more pay than is offered would be unspeakable. Generally speaking, women are not as aggressive as men.

The leading practice in pay is don't negotiate. Everyone gets hired at the same pay for the same job. No negotiation means everyone is treated equitably. At CCDI, we conduct a job assessment when we're creating a new role and when responsibilities change. Roles have different levels, and the level of a role defines its salary. Everyone who comes in as a manager makes the same amount, likewise senior managers, and so on. We include salaries as part of job descriptions so that everyone knows what the job pays and there isn't a salary range.

The Holy Grail of Hiring

Every organization is looking for the holy grail of hiring, the perfect process to ensure acquiring the best talent. But, truth time: the perfect process simply doesn't exist. As you can see, there are myriad potential barriers in the hiring process. The first step in attracting different talent is to ensure your process is inclusive. That starts with the language in the job posting, where it's posted, how candidates are screened and interviewed, and how they're hired. Every stage of the process sends a message. For example, when someone applies for a job, do you acknowledge the application? Do you inform people who have applied that they didn't get chosen for an interview? If you don't, what message are you sending? I'll let you in on a secret: it's not a good impression. And before you say, "We don't have the time," I say all you need to do is send a bulk e-mail, not handwritten notes.

I'll say this about name-blind hiring: it has been talked about for years as a way to address bias in the hiring process. People point back to the 1970s, when orchestras changed the audition process so that performers auditioned from behind a screen.[2] The result was that a significant number of women musicians landed jobs in orchestras, as the decision was based solely on an artist's ability to play. That worked for orchestras, because even if the conductor was a rabid sexist, the hiring process considered only the musician's work product. But name-blind hiring won't work for most organizations, because even if you take the name off the résumé, there are two subsequent problems.

First, lots can be gleaned about a person from a résumé: membership in a club might suggest they're a woman or LGBTQ2+; their graduation year or length of employment might indicate age; or a previous employer can suggest that they're a newcomer. If you want to figure it out, you can. Second, if you have a bias against a particular group—let's say black people, for this example—when the candidate walks in the room, they're still going to be black. So now the person has made it through the résumé screening and possibly a phone screening, but they don't get past the first interview. It's even worse if the interviewer says something like, "Oh, I didn't think you'd be black." Insert head-slap emoji.

Addressing bias in the hiring process by educating recruiters and hiring managers to spot it in themselves is far more effective than name-blind hiring. Ensuring that your process has mechanisms in place to address bias when it occurs—such as conducting panel interviews as opposed to one-on-one, and using a scoring rubric—is the best approach (because you're never going to have a bias-free process).

Strategies to Attract More, Different Talent

Now that you've reimagined your recruiting process, let's look at some ways to specifically attract different talent. One note: what follows isn't a definitive, all-encompassing list. It's a compilation of ideas that I've seen work effectively in other organizations. As you continue on your D&I journey, and as our societies change, you may discover other effective tactics for attracting difference.

A Thousand Words Paint a Picture

You now know how rife with issues job postings can be and that the language you use in your job postings can significantly influence who applies for your opening. Leading practices can help you avoid the pitfalls:

- Use software like Gender Decoder for Job Ads (free) or Textio (paid) to review the language in your job posting. These tools will highlight if you're using language that is coded for one sex over another.

- Ensure that you include only bona fide occupational requirements. Remove any "requirements" that aren't actually needed.

- Create a list of "must-haves" and "nice to haves." An unsubstantiated rumor purports that women will apply for a job only when they meet 100 percent of its qualification requirements, whereas men will apply if they have 60 percent. Even if this rumor, which has reached mythical proportions, is close to true, changing the list of requirements so that it is split between "we absolutely need this" and "we'd really love it if you also had this, but if you don't, please still apply," you may see an increase in the number of women applying.

- Make sure you can measure every requirement. How are you going to determine if someone is a "good team player"? If you can't measure it, remove it from the posting.

- Have people from the communities that you want to attract review the posting: women, newcomers, Indigenous people, and so on. They might see something in the posting that would be *less* attractive to their community and might be counter to what you're trying to achieve.

Finally, take note about "Canadian/US experience." As I mentioned previously, most (if not all) newcomers have heard the phrase "you don't have any Canadian/US experience" to explain why they're not right for a job. This is what I like to call "horse excrement." The value of "Canadian experience" or "American experience" is mythical. I've lived in other parts of the world and have never heard anyone say, "But you don't have any [insert country] experience."

Sometimes country-specific experience matters; for example, if the job requires you to be intimately familiar with the US tax code, then you need that experience. But most jobs don't require country-specific experience. If you're a brick-layer, bricks lay the same way in Japan as they do in Canada. Yes, some information will be new, but that can be learned. This rule applies to very few jobs, however, and so this excuse needs to stop. It disincentivizes newcomers, it gives organizations a bad reputation, and it's illegal (at least in Ontario).[3]

I challenge any employer to explain to me why their job requires Canadian or US experience, and I'd bet money that I can prove them wrong. (The money referred to here isn't real, and I'm not actually betting anyone. Just making a point.)

Find a Different Fishing Hole

To attract different talent, you need to post in different places. If you're just using Indeed, you're getting only people who look at Indeed. There are lots of different places you can post your job, which will ultimately attract different talent. For example, have you considered sending your postings to immigrant-serving agencies? Thousands of organizations exist to help newcomers integrate, which includes finding a job (there are sixty in Toronto alone). Send them your job posting, and they will send you some exceptional talent. What about women's industry groups, like Women in Mining or the South Asian Bar Association? There are literally thousands of such groups, some of them small and niche, and some of them quite large.

If you specifically want to target a particular demographic, you need to go where that talent is. You don't need to change your recruiting process. People can still apply through your ATS, but give agencies or groups a referral code so, at the very least, you'll look at the résumés that come through them. Casting a wider net will help you target talent that isn't looking at Indeed.

Take It to the People

If you want to attract people from a particular community, you need to let that community know that you're open for business. Don't assume that posting a sentence on a job description like "our organization is an equal-opportunity employer" is going to encourage anyone to click *submit*. That statement means nothing. In fact, people see through it as dated language.

The challenge for most employers is that they're competing with some massive brands that people aspire to work for. The best way to compete is to get out there and let people know you're there. Going to cultural festivals—whether a Cinco de Mayo event, a Diwali celebration, or another occasion—will send a message that you're serious about hiring from that community.

Every community has festivals, which are a great way to connect. For example, there are more than three hundred LGBTQ2+ Pride festivals across North America every year. If you want to attract LGBTQ2+ people and their allies, attending is a good way to get your name out there. But don't do interviews at your booth. When people are celebrating, they have no interest in sitting down for a chat about job opportunities. And do yourself a favor: don't print a takeaway card or flyer. The vast majority will end up in the bin, and you'll have hurt Mother Nature. Have a purpose for your booth—such as, if they sign up for a mailing list, they'll get a chance to win a prize. That way you'll get people's e-mail addresses, Twitter handles, cell numbers, or whatever, and you can send them *one* (and I do mean only one) message afterward, pointing them in the direction of your open postings.

Back to Basics

Recruiters will be cursing my name for this one, because they hate job fairs. The problem recruiters have with job fairs is that they stand there all day and talk to people and then tell them to apply online. They might take someone's résumé, but the exchange will likely go nowhere. The days of recruiters working intimately with candidates is long gone. Whereas twenty years ago they might have had ten open positions, they now have more than thirty open positions at any one time and don't have the capacity to do anything outside the basic process.

But the tried-and-true job fair can be effective—if you do it *right*. Done properly, recruiting events can be a great source of different talent. But what does "right" look like? Here's an idea. Conduct real interviews, on the spot:

- Start with a prescreening interview (this can take less than ten minutes) to get a sense of whether the candidate has any of the skills you're looking for. If they don't, thank them and encourage them to keep looking at your website.

- If you discover someone with potential, pass them on to a recruiter (also at the booth) who can interview them more formally to assess further.

- If the candidate passes that stage, ask them to apply online for the position you think they're right for (either at a workstation or tablet at your booth, or from home), and give them a referral code so you can guarantee they will get to the next phase.

Job seekers who go to these events are actively looking for work. They don't need a pen or a coffee mug. They need a job in their chosen profession. Giving them an experience that shows you're genuinely interested in hiring people from their community will go a long way to building loyalty, and chances are you'll find an amazing hire in the bunch.

Spend Some Coin

If you want to recruit from a particular community, advertising and sponsorship works (if you've got money to spend). You can advertise in specific ethnocultural media or on billboards and in transit shelters in specific geographies; you can sponsor events like LGBTQ2+ Pride or targeted sports teams or events. There is an endless list of places where you can spend money that will send a message that you want to attract talent from a particular community. It doesn't have to be a lot of cash, but if appealing to different talent is a priority of your organization, you should be able to find a few pennies to put your name on a banner. Instead of sponsoring a golf tournament, why not spend a few dollars where it's going to have a bigger impact?

Key Takeaways

- Look at your hiring process and do your best to remove as much of the potential bias as possible.

- Name-blind hiring isn't a solution to address bias. D&I training is.

- To attract difference, reach beyond your traditional process to post jobs in different places, do outreach to communities, use job fairs effectively, and spend money where it will count the most.

Enjoying the book?

Why not leave a review with your favorite book seller

★ ★ ★ ★ ★

If you're not enjoying it... why are you still reading it?
Nothing left to watch on Netflix?

7

DEVELOPING YOUR PEOPLE

Talent development, talent advancement, succession planning—whatever you call it, the point is the same: What are you doing to develop your people so that they stay with you longer and advance in their careers?

Developing your talent is not about being a nice employer. It's about being a smart employer. The longer a person stays with you, the more value you get from them. From the moment you hire someone, you're investing in them. Seeing the return on that investment takes time. The more you invest, the bigger your return.

Development isn't always planned, and it's never equitable. I know that's a bold statement to make, but it's true. Not everyone receives the same opportunity as everyone else, and not everyone *deserves* the same opportunity as everyone else. Not everyone has the same ability as everyone else. But how are you determining who deserves development? Further, are you taking diversity into consideration when you are deciding who gets that development?

Many organizations have a "hi-po," or high potential, list—a list of people in the organization who are believed to have the potential to be promoted into bigger roles. How many of those organizations can explain how someone gets on or off that list? Not many. I've observed that managers always determine whether one of their direct reports, some-one they deem as promotion-worthy, should be on the hi-po list. Then the identified person does something (or doesn't do something), and they're taken off the list. At no point is the person aware that they were on the hi-po list, or that they were being watched. Does that seem like a recipe for success? (The correct response is, "No, Michael, it doesn't.") It's a bit creepy, when you think about it.

Studies have shown a lot of differences between men and women and the way they succeed. For example, in the book *Women Don't Ask: Negotiation and the Gender Divide*, the authors, Linda Babcock and Sara Laschever, found that men are four times more likely than women to ask for a raise; and when women do ask for a pay increase, they typically request 30 percent less than men do.[1] There are other considerations. For example, people from different cultural backgrounds, particularly those raised outside North America, may have a different understanding of workplace etiquette and norms. For some people, expressing interest in a promotion or advancement opportunity would be completely unacceptable.

Their expectation may be that they will do a good job and be identified as worthy of the opportunity. Just because they don't ask for it doesn't mean they're not interested. But in the end, the squeaky wheel gets the cheese. Or whatever you do with squeaky wheels. Or cheese.

When looking at the advancement of your people, particularly when you intend to diversify your leadership, there are several factors to consider. Let's take a look.

Define Success Differently

The first thing to understand is that not everyone wants to be king. I have been in workplaces where it's assumed that everyone wants to be promoted. That's just not so. You don't know what's going on in everyone's life. You have no idea what a person's motivations are. Some people definitely want to advance in their careers. Some are quite happy going to work and doing their job, and they're not interested in climbing the ladder. Many years ago I was at a meeting with a woman who was an incredible hi-po, but she didn't want to be promoted. I bluntly asked her why. She was equally blunt in her response. As she put it, she had a young family and no interest in dealing with the headaches that came with leadership. She saw what promotions did to some people, and although the money would be nice, the price of admission was too great. She was content in her role and didn't need more.

Some employers speak of "career managers" (people who reach a certain level within the organization and then don't have the skill or desire to progress any further), and in an "up or out" culture, this *isn't* a positive label. But not everyone can be promoted, right? And we still need managers to do the work, correct? There's nothing wrong with a career manager. In fact, we need them. Not everyone is going to be CEO. We need people to do the work, and being a manager (or whatever title) for a prolonged period is great, provided the person is deciding that for themselves and you're not choosing it for them. If a person doesn't have the skills to advance to the next level, that's a different conversation. Which leads me to...

Talk to Your People

Here's a radical concept: talk to your people. How "out there" is that?! What I mean is, the best way to determine if someone is a hi-po is by asking them what they aspire to. Having productive performance management conversations is hard at times, but it's far better to address things than leave them to chance.

The leading practice is to sit down with each of your direct reports and ask the age-old question: "Where do you see yourself in five years?" The answer might surprise you. The person who you thought was a hi-po might say, "I want to be a Pilates instructor." If you're an engineering firm, that person might not be a good fit for a promotion. That said, the person whom you didn't see as wanting a promotion might then say, "I want *your* job." Give your people the latitude to tell you what they want. Don't assume anything. Allow them to express their interest and then deal with it.

It's All in How You Say It

Asking a person about their career aspirations does not establish a legal precedent. Telling them they're going to get promoted and then not promoting them? That's a legal pickle right there.

However, you can say things like, "I can't guarantee anything," and that makes it clear that you're not committing to a promotion. Manage their expectations throughout the process and you won't find yourself in court.

Be Honest

Some people have such a hard time with honesty. They don't want to hurt anyone's feelings. Well, your lack of honesty may have a bigger impact than a few hurt feelings. If someone expresses interest in a promotion and they don't have the potential, you owe it to them to be honest about it. You don't have to be mean. But you can say, "I appreciate your interest, but that won't be possible."

Then you have to explain why. And you'd better have a good reason. For example, if your administrative assistant wants to be doing audits, your reasoning might be that to do an audit, you need to be a CPA (Chartered Professional Account). That's a bona fide occupational requirement. There's no getting around that. But if that same administrative assistant wants to be in sales, what's your excuse? Just because you can't imagine them in sales doesn't mean they wouldn't be a sales rock star.

Be honest—and base that honesty in fact, not fiction. I once worked with a client that had an employee who lived with extreme epilepsy. The employer had done everything to accommodate this person, based on advice from a prominent epilepsy organization. Truthfully, the employer was bending over backward to create space for this individual—not because he was good at his job, but because the employer was terrified that they would be perceived as not inclusive. But at the end of the day, he did not have the skills required to do the job. And that's okay. His lack of skill had nothing to do with his epilepsy. The employer's mistake was trying to avoid the thousand-pound gorilla in the room. This person should've been managed out of his role and not encouraged to do something he simply didn't have the skills for.

Make a Plan

Development doesn't happen magically. You need to be deliberate. There needs to be a plan. If someone just told you they want to be promoted, say from manager to senior manager, what is the plan to get them there? What skills and experience do they need to make that promotion possible? What's the difference in skills and experience between a manager and a senior manager? You need to be able to articulate that and then create a plan to help the person get the skills and experience they need to achieve the promotion.

Take Ownership

Both of you must take ownership. Once you have a plan, it's up to both of you to take ownership of it to ensure its success. Yes, each person needs to own their own career trajectory, but as their manager, if they're heading in the wrong direction or not achieving the goals, you owe it to them to help fix that.

Skills and Personality Traits

Understand the difference between a skill and a personality trait. You also can't just say, "You need to be more outgoing." Being outgoing isn't a skill that you can teach or learn. Either you are outgoing or you're not. This is where we start to get into the difference between extroverts and introverts, between which there are some key differences. Here are just a few, outlined by Susan Cain in her book *Quiet: The Power of Introverts in a World that Can't Stop Talking*:

- Extroverts recharge by being social; introverts recharge when they're alone.

- Extroverts tend to tackle projects quickly, make quick decisions, and take risks; introverts work slowly and deliberately, focus on one task at a time, and can concentrate to no end.

- Those talkative extroverts tend to be assertive and outspoken, and they crave company and attention (they're the life of the party, or the meeting). Introverts may or may not like a party or a meeting, but they'll eventually need to recharge; they prefer to listen than to talk, and they prefer the company of a few close friends or allies to big, stimulating groups.

- Extroverts are unphased by conflict; introverts not so much.[2]

These are generalizations, and some people are "cuspers" (also, but not widely, known as ambiverts), meaning they have traits of both. I myself am an extrovert on the cusp of introvert. I can give an amazing, high energy, entertaining speech or presentation (they really are all that), but I recharge by going home and cuddling my dog.

If you think of these traits as they relate to promoting people, you can see that some skills will be easy for a person to pick up, and some will be incredibly hard. It all depends on their personality type. When you're determining the skills and abilities required for a promotion, you need to identify the bona fide occupational requirements: What is *really* needed to do the job?

Some personality traits are, in fact, bona fide occupational requirements. Consider litigators, the lawyers that argue. Their job is to confront and challenge. A person who avoids confrontation would be a terrible litigator because the entire job is confrontation. However, many personality traits are not required skills for particular roles. Whether you make decisions quickly or take a while to reflect before deciding may have no bearing on your capacity as an accountant, as long as the decisions are sound. Why would a long-haul trucker need to be friendly and outgoing? Knowing the difference between what is and isn't required is vital.

Practice the Platinum Rule

The platinum rule is a variation on the Golden Rule: "Do unto others as you would have others do unto you." Every religion or faith on the planet has some version of the Golden Rule, regardless of what it is called, but there's a problem with it: It assumes the other person wants or needs to be treated the same way as you. This is why I invite you to upgrade to platinum: "Treat others the way *they* would like to be treated."[3] Look at the concept of face time as an example (face time as in being face-to-face, not as in FaceTime, the video conferencing software). In many Asian countries, face time with your boss is viewed as a reward, yet in North America, we're actively trying to do away with the need for face-to-face interaction. So which practice is right? Both, and neither. But knowing that, if you have an employee who recently emigrated from South Korea, making a point of giving them some face time will build loyalty and engagement.

Treat people how they need to be treated, not how you think they need to be treated. Thinking back to the difference between equality and equity, which we discussed in chapter 1, the Golden Rule describes equality (treating everyone the same); the platinum rule describes equity (treating someone how they need to be treated). I cannot overemphasize the importance of this in talent development. Not everyone has the same needs, so why would you treat everyone the same?

If a woman has a baby and takes a year or more off work, that affects her career progression. She doesn't lose her skills. She loses time. In professions that have a clear path of development based on time (such as accounting or law, where most people enter the profession as students and progress with their "class" at the same rate), a year off means that woman *may* not be at the same place as her peers when she comes back to work. Of course, she may return and be such a rock star that she keeps step with peers. Or not. Each situation is different. And the same would be the case for a man who took a year off for paternity leave, or for any reason at all.

The important consideration is to treat individuals based on their own needs and abilities. Continuing on this example, when our woman lawyer/accountant is having a baby, there are a few things to consider:

- How long does she want to go on leave for, regardless of how long she's legally entitled to take?

- What does her off-boarding process look like? Who's taking over her workload in her absence?

- What does her reintegration look like? Does she want to do a gradual return to work (aka part-time for a period before returning to full-time)?

- Have her career aspirations changed while she was on leave?

- What can you do, once she's back to full-time, to get her back on track?

You have to think about the needs of the individual, you have to talk to the person, and you have to plan.

Be Targeted

You may be thinking that most of this chapter has been about really good people management, and not about diversity and inclusion. That's what I like to call "correct." Until now. At some point you may look at your leadership and determine that you need to be more targeted about promotions. That point is usually when you realize your leadership is, to describe it politely, "pale, stale, and male." I didn't come up with that phrase, so don't hate me. A guy named Daniel Goldin coined it in 1992 when describing NASA's administration. Blame him. I use it because, as you know by now, I love a good rhyme.

Goldin noted that NASA's administration was dominated by SWAMs and that the organization lacked the diversity that ultimately drives innovation. You might see that in the leadership of your organization too. Hence, you may find yourself needing to be targeted. Being targeted is a good thing, and it's not reverse discrimination (remember, there's no such thing). Being targeted levels the playing field.

I'll use an example of an organization that suspected a leak in the pipeline for women and people of color, and they noticed that these groups weren't progressing into leadership at the same rate as white men. After a lengthy study of the data, the leadership realized that a slightly higher percentage of women and people of color were leaving the organization and not being promoted, in comparison to white men.

The more junior ranks of the organization had gender parity—in fact, women were the majority—as well as a significantly higher level of ethnocultural diversity. But going up the ranks, the gender parity vanished, and so did the ethnocultural difference. Through anecdotal conversations, women and people of color expressed (among other things) that they didn't see themselves having the opportunity, and so they looked elsewhere.

To address the situation and ensure the organization was *actually* promoting the best and brightest, the leadership put a particular focus on the development of women and people of color. That involved these groups being targeted. They looked at the women and people of color on the hi-po list and determined what each individual needed to make it to the next stage of their career. They saw the need for things like mentors, sponsors, client opportunities, challenging projects, and so on, and then tailored the support to help each get to the next level.

No one was guaranteed a promotion. Far from it. People had to prove, just like anyone else, that they were up to the job. But the company's leadership accepted the reality that some people (usually SWAMs) were already getting the help they needed to advance their careers. They made sure that from then on, everyone was treated equitably.

Not everyone is jumping up and down asking for a promotion, but that doesn't mean that the people quietly doing their jobs don't want to move up. To diversify your leadership, you may have to take some deliberate action that has you targeting specific groups for development.

Key Takeaways

- Talent development needs to be deliberate and well-thought-out.

- Talk to your people and find out what they want, as opposed to what you think they want.

- Be deliberate and targeted to support development of your people and difference in your leadership.

MEASUREMENT FOR SUCCESS

worked for accountants for the better part of a decade, so I freely admit that I have a bias toward measurement. However, regardless of that admission, I can't emphasize enough the importance of measurement in assessing your diversity and inclusion efforts. Imagine a company that wants to create a blueberry chocolate bar (which I think sounds delicious, so Mars—step it up). To start, the company would do a huge amount of research and development, as well as marketing and product testing. Upon launching, they would invest a load of money into marketing to ensure success. And then they would . . . guess if they were successful? No! They would measure the product within an inch of its life to know if it was a success.

In case you missed the point: How do you know if you're making any difference if you're not measuring? D&I work is all about change of some kind, and that change should be measured. So, let's look at what you can measure and how often you should measure.

Measuring Diversity

Measuring diversity is slightly easier than measuring inclusion, because it involves more concrete numbers, which is far simpler and easier to understand than measuring the qualitative data on inclusion. Diversity is a quantitative measurement. There's no interpretation involved. Either you do or you don't. Measuring diversity breaks down into two different categories:

Demographic Representation

Collecting demographic information (such as ethnocultural identity, sexual orientation, disability, etc.) is *not* a leading D&I practice so much as it is table stakes. Category 8 of the Global Diversity and Inclusion Benchmarks (GDIB)—Assessment, Measurement, and Research—indicates that measuring your diversity by asking people to self-identify by demographic information falls somewhere between reactive and proactive.[1] But if you're not doing it, you're likely not doing much else—or at least not much else that is affecting change. Again, how do you know if you have gaps in your representation if you don't know what your representation is?

I've heard every excuse in the book about why an employer *can't* collect demographic information, none of which holds water. Usually the reality of the situation is that employers are afraid of asking because they're scared of what they'll find out. So, let's address a few questions I get asked frequently about collecting demographic information from your people.

One important note before we begin: the responses to the questions below are based on my understanding of the laws in Canada and the United States. As much as I played a lawyer on TV once (you can Google that little treat), I strongly encourage you to verify this with a lawyer licensed in your specific geography.

Is it legal to ask these questions?

The answer varies based on the country, but in Canada and the United States, yes, it is completely legal to ask these questions. You can ask anything you like, provided that:

The user can opt out of responding. You can make it mandatory to respond to a census, but people must be able to opt out of answering the questions. I strongly recommend that every question have a "prefer not to answer" option as opposed to an "opt out" for the entire census. Humans are lazy. If you allow people to opt out, they will. Not because they don't want to answer, but because they're lazy! (Or they may be busy doing their job or whatever.) In my experience, a very small percentage of participants (less than 1 percent on average) will select "prefer not to answer" on every question. The highest percentage of "prefer not to answer" (in the double digits) always relates to age, followed by sexual orientation and religion (each in the single digits).

There's a crystal-clear privacy statement. You must explain who will have access to the data, whether or not it's anonymous (but results *should* be anonymous), where the data is stored (on a server located in Canada, the United States, or somewhere else), and exactly what the data will be used for.

It doesn't impact employment. You must ensure the data isn't used against a person. For example, if a person self-identifies as living with mental illness, you can't remove that person from their job because of it. That would be discrimination. This is very important to note so that you don't have a manager with an explicit bias against one group using information to exclude someone because they found out that one of their team is "x."

Can't I just guess? I can clearly see this person is [fill in identity here].
In the United States, you can guess (and you are required to guess if a person doesn't self-identify), but I really don't suggest it. In Canada, it's absolutely a no-no. The term is "*self*-identification." You don't get to decide how your people identify. They do. If a person who is "clearly" South Asian (as far as you're concerned) does not self-identify as such, that's up to them.

This question comes up a lot, particularly with regard to people living with disabilities, with employers that are subject to legislation—specifically, when the employer provides an accommodation related to an employee's disability, yet the employee doesn't tick that box. The same goes for Indigenous people and people of color when the employer is trying to improve their representation numbers because they're required to by law. I hear it all the time: "The person is clearly black [or East Asian, or a lesbian, or...]. Can't I just count them?"

I know it's a pain. I get it. But that's life. The onus is on the employer to create a space where people understand why it's helpful for their employer to have that information. If the employee doesn't tick the box, you should be asking why not. What are their reasons? What can you do, as the employer, to create a space that encourages honest self-identification?

The caveat to this is that in the United States, where employers are required to provide the demographic information about all employees to the government, if they haven't self-identified, then you have to guess. I don't like this, but if you have to do it, you must.

I already know their sex and age. Do I need anything more?
Okay, so let me guess how you have that information: you collected it at onboarding. And as part of that collection, did you tell your employees that you were going to use that information for the purposes that you're using it? There's the rub.

Canada's privacy legislations (both federally and provincially) stipulate that you have to tell a person what you're going to do with any personal information that you collect. When a person is onboarded, you collect their sex and age as part of requirements under provincial and federal labor laws. I have never seen an employer provide a privacy statement that tells the employee that the information will be used to calculate the representation of the organization, or any other usage related to D&I. *If you don't have that privacy statement, it's as if you don't have the information.*

Organizations in the United States are not subject to this legislation, but American readers should keep privacy in mind if they are dealing with employees in different countries, such as Canada.

How many questions should we ask?
Truthfully, this is up to you. You could follow your local legislation and ask the questions specific to the law. My issues with asking questions based solely on the law are twofold:

The questions tend to be limited. The experiences of one group are vastly different from another, even if they're in the same bucket, such as people of color, LGBTQ2+, or people living with disabilities. I live with chronic depression, but my experience in employment is nowhere near the same as a person who uses a wheelchair. Yet we're both part of the "disability" bucket. The same is the case for people of color. There's a hierarchy within each group. The broad buckets don't give you enough information to do anything.

The questions are exclusionary. If you're an able-bodied white man, on most legislatively led surveys, there isn't a box for you. To me, that has always seemed pretty contradictory to the concept of inclusion. When I first introduced data collection at a former employer (years ahead of most other employers at the time), I made sure that every single person had a box to tick. Even SWAMs. They need to be included too. Again, we're not talking about marginalization and underrepresentation. But to move from the social justice model of D&I to the creativity and innovation model, we need to make sure everyone feels like they matter.

The leading practice is to go beyond what you are legally required to ask, to be more inclusive. Include questions about sex (where males are counted too) and gender/gender identity (these are separate questions), sexual orientation, religion, and so much more.

What if I'm curious about . . . ?

There's an old proverb: curiosity killed the cat.[2] While I love an old proverb, your curiosity isn't a good enough reason to ask questions. The number one rule in collecting personal demographic information is that you need to have a purpose for asking for said information. What are you going to do with it? Why does it matter that you have the information? How are you going to change things in your workplace based on this information? You need a purpose. And if you don't have one, don't ask the question!

What about collecting using a free survey tool?

Nothing inspires confidence and says "professional" like a free survey tool. No offence meant, but aside from appearing a tad unprofessional, it's better to avoid free survey tools, for a few different reasons.

First, if you use a US company with servers based in the United States, the data is subject to the Patriot Act. If you're not familiar with it, the US Patriot Act is a sweeping piece of legislation that was brought in after the 9/11 tragedy, and it gives the government a lot of power. Employers need to think about where their data is stored and what laws that data is subject to. Canada's privacy laws are strict, and using a server located in Canada subjects the data to Canadian laws.

Second, online survey tools are not truly anonymous, because they collect one form of personal information: an IP address. This is basically a digital fingerprint. When using online survey tools, you can't avoid that, so you can't assure your people that the census is completely anonymous.

Third, with a free online tool, you can't track year to year without asking for a personal identifier. If you want to track the progress of people through promotions, for example, you will have to ask them to include a personal identifier, such as their name or employee ID. If you have that, you'll be able to see how each person self-identifies. Not a good idea. But if you keep things truly anonymous, you won't be able to tell what changes have occurred, because you won't know who participated from one year to the next. The information will essentially be brand-new every year.

If you really want to use a simple survey tool (for instance, if you're a small employer and don't have your own human resources information system or the budget to hire an outside consultant), at the very least look for one that takes privacy into consideration, and be very careful about how you structure the census.

Going beyond Representation

Your representation is one thing, but to understand if you're making progress, you could measure so many additional elements:

Demographics of applicants, throughout the recruiting process. Who applies for jobs at your organization? Who gets screened in, who gets a phone interview, and who gets an in-person interview? Who gets hired? Tracking the candidates throughout the process will show you if there's an issue with your recruiting. Ideally, the representation should stay consistent at every step. In reality, that is rarely the case. For example, if half of the applicants for a job are women and half are men, does that stay consistent throughout the hiring process? Theoretically, it should. But if it doesn't, where does it fall apart, and why? Knowing this will help you change your recruiting process so that you hire the best and the brightest.

Demographics and performance ratings. Everyone gets treated fairly in performance ratings, right? (If you believe that, you'd believe me if I said I have an oil for sale that will cure literally anything and make you more attractive.) Wrong. It's not true. The performance rating process is rife with potential bias. The only way to identify where that bias comes into play is by comparing the demographic representation against performance ratings to see if certain groups tend to do better than others.

Demographics and promotions. According to CCDI's research, in the legal profession in 2016, 54.67 percent of articling or summer students identified as female, yet only 24.64 percent of equity partners identify as female.[3] Does that mean that the women who articled in 2006 (ten years is the average time to get from being called to the Bar to partner) just weren't good enough to make partner, even though they made up more than half of the potential candidates? The answer is no. And before you think, "Well, it's just going to take time," these numbers have remained relatively flat for more than twenty years. Women in the legal profession have been overlooked for promotion and ultimately have had to move on to move up. And the legal profession isn't the exception to the rule. Most industries face the same issue. To combat this, demographics must be included in the promotion process to ensure bias isn't affecting the outcome. Without looking at the demographics, you wouldn't know if the people being promoted are reflective of the pipeline of talent.

Demographics and pay. This is always a sticky one. Most employers genuinely believe that they pay people the same for equal work. This is what I like to call "delusional." We have more than enough data to show that women are consistently paid less for the same work in comparison to their male counterparts. Both Canada and the United States have the eighth-highest gender pay gap out of forty-three countries examined by the Organization for Economic Cooperation and Development (OECD), with women making about $0.78 for every dollar made by a man.[4] If you know there is a wage gap for women, have you considered looking at it through any other demographic lens, such as by ethnicity or ability? It stands to reason that there may be a gap.

Measuring Inclusion

Truthfully, measuring inclusion is a little more difficult because it's not as clear-cut as diversity. Inclusion can be open to interpretation, but you can still measure qualitatively.

Inclusion or Engagement Survey

Everyone's favorite measurement mechanism is the tried-and-true survey. You can either conduct a stand-alone inclusion survey or you can integrate inclusion questions into your existing engagement survey. You don't need a lot. Four or five questions can tell you a lot about how included people feel. For example, you could consider including statements such as, "Leadership in my organization is committed to diversity and inclusion" or "At my organization, I feel included."

The important part of the process is to cross-segment the response by demographics; otherwise, you'll mask the reality of the situation. Let's look at an example. Consider the statement "I feel valued at work." Assuming a relative balance of women and men (apart from those identifying by another gender) in the respondent pool, if the positive sentiment is 80 percent, that's a great result, right? Maybe. But what if, when we look more closely, we find that men responded with a positive sentiment of 90 percent and women with a positive sentiment of 70 percent? While 70 percent isn't a bad score, 20 percent is an enormous gap where the respondent groups are similar in size. That tells us that women and men are experiencing the organization in different ways. In this case, women do not feel as valued as men.

Inclusion surveys are meant to tell you if people are feeling included, and to identify where one group feels more or less included than another. Then you must try to understand why that is. I've always said that this type of survey doesn't tell you why there's a fire, but it tells you where to point your hose.

Focus Groups

An inclusion survey may tell you there's an issue with a particular group, but it won't tell you why. Focus groups are a great way to ask questions and get some honest feedback.

Although there are lots of ways to run focus groups, the leading practice is to have an external third party do them. People will be far more honest with a stranger than with a colleague or boss. It's also best to conduct focus groups virtually, especially when there are issues with the culture. In my experience, where the culture is bad, people will happily participate in focus groups, but they won't say a word in person, even when the focus group is conducted by a third party. People open up more truthfully when they can share their thoughts without having anyone hear them speak.

One-On-One Interviews

Similar to focus groups, one-on-one interviews are a great way to gather feedback. At CCDI, we use these specifically when gathering feedback from leaders, but they work for any group. Again, these are better done by an external party providing a safe space where a person can share thoughts without fear of repercussions.

Assessment

Now comes the fancy part. You've got a bunch of data from your diversity and inclusion measurements, and you need to devise an assessment. Think of it like telling a story. What does the data tell you? The professionals use a process called triangulation, which "refers to the practice of using multiple sources of data or multiple approaches to analyzing data to enhance the credibility of a research study."[5] If you didn't know the word, it's unlikely you know how to do it, so you may want to hire one of those experts to do the analysis. The assessment will reveal the issues: who your people are, and who your people should be (based on available sources of data on talent), as well as how your people feel as it relates to the inclusiveness of the organization.

From the assessment, you can build your diversity and inclusion strategy to address the identified issues. This data collection and assessment process should be conducted every three to five years—first at the beginning of your journey and then as you progress along your journey, to determine if your efforts are having the intended impact. If you've identified a lack of diversity in the pipeline for leadership, and your solution involves multiple actions—changing the recruiting process, creating a talent development program for under-represented groups, and so on—then you'll want to know if your efforts have addressed the issues, which goes beyond just looking at the representation of your leadership.

Measuring Maturity

Thanks to decades of research, we now understand what an organization looks like when it's more "mature" in diversity and inclusion. Measuring organizational maturity is about determining where you are based on a generally accepted set of conditions, which gives you a clearer road map for your D&I journey. Measuring maturity is a burgeoning area of practice that is receiving more focus than ever, but it is still developing. The GDIB (Global Diversity and Inclusion Benchmarks) is a relatively good starting point. It has four-teen categories—everything from vision and leadership to marketing and supplier diversity—and within each there are a total of 266 benchmarks at five different levels of maturity. In essence, it evaluates an organization from a policy and program perspective. It defines leading and lagging indicators, so you can determine where you should be, theoretically, based on whether or not you have those things. "Leading indicators" are those famous leading practices that put you at the front of the pack, as opposed to the "lagging indicators" that place you at the back. For example, the GDIB clearly states that diversity councils chaired by the most senior person in an organization (or one of their direct reports) have far more influence than those chaired by someone else. As such, if your diversity council is chaired by someone other than the most senior person in your organization, it logically stands that you are not as mature in your D&I journey.

Industry Benchmarking

Measuring the diversity and inclusion of your industry is a bit tricky, but it can be done. In essence, you create a benchmark by examining your competitors or similar organizations to understand what and how they're doing in the area of diversity and inclusion. You can do this in one or both of two ways. You can examine publicly available information. What explicit information about diversity and inclusion is on the competition's websites, in reports, and in other publications, such as government websites, if the organization is subject to legislation? What implicit information is available, such as images on their website? What messages do their marketing materials send?

You can also ask directly. This involves contacting the organization and interviewing the person responsible for diversity and inclusion (the person who chairs the diversity council, if it exists, or if all else fails, someone in HR). To get an accurate comparison, ask a standard set of questions, such as what their annual D&I budget is, and how many full- or part-time resources are working in D&I. The questions will depend on what you're trying to find out. However, this technique works best when conducted by a third party that commits to keeping the information confidential, and where a copy of the results is provided back to the organizations interviewed.

When choosing whom to compare yourself against, it's crucial that you choose organizations that are very similar to yours. A national bank would compare itself to other national banks. A municipal police service would compare itself to police services of a proportional size in similar communities. The New York Police Department would want to compare itself to police services in Los Angeles and Atlanta, not Des Moines, where the size of the service and the community are vastly different.

Measuring Return on Investment

You must ensure that diversity and inclusion work is sustained by continually proving the value it brings to your organization. If you stop proving it, your organization will stop prioritizing it. Therefore, the return on investment (ROI) of D&I is the holy grail of measurement. And it's been elusive—until now.

Measuring the ROI of D&I is about connecting the dots. I'll give you an example.

Let's say you've done your assessment and strategy, so you know where the issues lie, and your organization decides to spend $200 per employee (per year for two years) on D&I programs focused on addressing those issues. In the grand scheme, $200 per person is not a lot of money, but let's go with it. And just because I like defined numbers, let's say you have a thousand people in your organization. So that's an annual budget of $200,000 for two years. That may or may not include salaries for full- or part-time resources working on D&I. It doesn't matter for this hypothesis.

After two years, you need to measure to determine the return on your $200,000 investment. Let's assume your assessment included an inclusion survey and/or engagement survey. So, as part of your measurement after the two years, you conduct the same survey and determine whether your scores have gone up or down. If you've done things right, your scores should go up. In this scenario, let's assume your engagement goes up by 10 percent, which is not outside of the realm of possibility. In fact, it's very conservative. (As I pointed out on page 60, Deloitte Australia's report "Waiter, Is That Inclusion in My Soup?" shows that organizations with a strong commitment to diversity, whose employees felt included, saw a lift of as much as 101 percent on engagement scores.[6]) According to Aon, the average employee engagement in Canada in 2018 was 69 percent.[7] So let's say your engagement is now at 79 percent.

Now, let's say that you use productivity to measure the financial impact of engagement. Note that you could include many different measures in your ROI calculation to show the financial impact of your investment, such as lower levels of absenteeism and presenteeism, fewer human rights complaints, fewer legal issues, improved customer service, lower levels of turnover, and so on. Hypothesize with me that a 10 percent increase in engagement equates to a 10 percent increase in productivity.[8] (I'm making these numbers up to prove a point. You'll have to do the heavy lifting to figure out your own ROI, or [shameless self-promotion] you can use CCDI's ROI Meter service.)

What is a 10 percent increase in productivity worth? A 2010 report by the US Bureau of Labor Statistics found that the average American worker produces a value of $57.54 per hour worth of goods and services.[9] Although we don't have a Canadian stat, let's assume it's the same for Canada. In this scenario, let's consider a person making $24.04 per hour (or the equivalent of $50,000 per year). And now it's time for some math. Please buckle your seat belt and keep your hands inside the ride:

- If your engagement score overall was 69 percent, it's now at 79 percent because of the work you've done in diversity and inclusion.

- If productivity was $57.54 per hour at 69 percent, productivity increases to $63.29 per hour at 79 percent.

- If a person earns $24.04 per hour, their positive output goes from $33.50 per hour to $39.25 per hour (subtract $24.04 from $57.54 and then from $63.29).

- That person is, therefore, responsible for positive output of $78,500 per year (assuming 40 hours a week, 50 weeks a year) compared to $67,000 per year before the increase in engagement. That's an increase of $11,500.

- With one thousand employees (all making the same amount), that's an increase in revenue of $11,500,000 per year.

So, for an investment of $200,000 per year for two years, you see an increase in productivity of $11.5 million or a 28.75 percent return on investment. Not bad.

Admittedly, I just made a whole bunch of stuff up. There is no world in which this is accurate (if only because there is no organization in North America of one thousand employees all making $50,000 per year). That's not the point.

You *can* measure your return on investment. It's complicated, but it can be done. And in doing so, you'll see the positive impact this work can have on your top and bottom lines. Yay math!

Key Takeaways

- You can and should measure diversity and inclusion, and there are many ways to do so.

- Measurement helps you understand whether or not your actions are having the intended impact.

- You need to measure regularly to understand your progress.

THE KEY INGREDIENTS

There are three key ingredients in the D&I space that need to be addressed; in no particular order, these include diversity councils, employee resource groups, and D&I practitioners.

Value of Diversity Councils

I'll start with diversity councils, which, in my opinion, are one of the most undervalued and underutilized resources in diversity and inclusion work. In 2017, CCDI released a guide called *Diversity and Inclusion Councils: Toolkit for Diversity and Inclusion Practitioners* as a way to help employers establish diversity councils that are effective at delivering change. As the toolkit describes:

Executive- or senior leadership–led diversity councils can go by many names: executive diversity council, enterprise diversity council, executive diversity taskforce, diversity strategy team, etc. Usually led by the Executive Director, Chairperson, CEO, Chief Human Resources Officer (CHRO) or Chief Diversity Officer (CDO), such councils are made up of senior vice presidents; vice presidents; organizational, business-unit heads; functional unit heads; division heads; or other high-level leaders from across the organization. In general, this council develops or validates the comprehensive, integrated diversity strategy that drives best practices, goals and objectives and monitors progress against goals and objectives.[1]

There are different types of councils. Some are internally focused, while some are externally focused. Some are geographically specific, while others are responsible for diversity enterprise-wide. But all of them are valuable.

Oftentimes, councils are the "doers," particularly in organizations that don't have full- or part-time resources dedicated to D&I (they should, but let's just skip that for now). In these cases, council members are the strategists and the executers. They put on the celebrations, deliver the training, and review the processes and procedures. It's often difficult to be both strategist and executer, but some make it work. Other times, councils are the "advisors," particularly in organizations that do have full- or part-time D&I resources. The council provides strategic advice and is the "voice of the organization," offering insight into how a strategy or specific initiative may resonate in the organization.

This is the most important value of either the doer or the advisor: to be the voice of the organization. More often than not, members of the diversity council don't have experience in D&I, other than their lived experience. Council members are volunteers, so they have "day jobs" within the organization, and that's a good thing.

As you know, diversity and inclusion is a change-management exercise. And in any such exercise, key stakeholders must be at the table to provide insight into how the proposed change is going to go over in different areas of the organization. A hospital's diversity council might introduce an open-plan workspace, but the doctors and nurses might not be down with that idea—and by the way, a Harvard study found that open-plan workspaces led to a decrease in collaboration.[2] Just saying.

The opportunity is to create a diversity council composed of representation from different areas of your organization, different levels within the hierarchy, as well as different personal-characteristic diversity. When putting together your council, keep three things in mind:

Who is on the council? Choose a diversity of voices and perspectives. You don't need a council of fifty people. You just need to think through who you invite to the table. Jenny Chan, a (hypothetical) manager from IT, can represent her department, her level, and her personal-characteristic diversity all in one. The leading practice here is to have an application process and ask people to apply. Consider this work a development opportunity, particularly because the members will get exposure to senior leadership. As part of the application, ask people to self-identify by different demographic categories. Then use that information as part of the decision-making process.

I don't recommend using a nominating process, as that allows for bias to come into play, and you will inevitably end up with one-sided diversity, meaning that no SWAMs will be put forward. To be completely inclusive, you need at least one SWAM.

Which leaders are involved? At the very least, the council needs an executive sponsor, who should be either the most senior person in the organization or one of their direct reports. That person needs to take accountability for the actions of the council, so they need to show up to the meetings to see what's happening. The leading practice I recommend is to have the council co-chaired by the most senior leader and someone a few levels below. The senior leader is there as the executive sponsor, and the other person is there to do the work. It's a great development opportunity—not only for the co-chair, but for every member of the council.

What is the purpose? Councils notoriously fall down when they don't have an instruction manual. Councils need to understand their purpose and scope. As such, they need a mission, a vision, and values; they need goals and objectives; and they need roles and responsibilities. It's critical that your council start off on the right foot by establishing the framework from which they will operate.

To learn more about setting up a diversity council for success, review CCDI's *Diversity and Inclusion Councils* toolkit, which you can download at https://ccdi.ca/toolkits/. If you do it correctly, a diversity council can be an incredible resource for the organization as it relates to executing on a diversity and inclusion strategy.

Value of Employee Resource Groups

An often-missing piece of the big D&I puzzle is employee resource groups. ERGs have been around since the 1960s, and they're an exceptional resource, if they're delivered properly.

The concept got its start from Joseph Wilson, the former CEO of Xerox, following race riots in Rochester, New York, in 1964. Wilson and his black employees designed and launched the National Black Employees Caucus in 1970 to address racial tension and issues of workplace discrimination.[3]

ERGs go by many names—business resource groups, associate resource groups, affinity networks—but they're all relatively the same at the end of the day: a group of volunteer employees who share a common dimension of diversity and who come together to provide support, education, or other offerings to the benefit of both the individuals and the employer. Women's ERGs, Pride (LGBTQ2+) ERGs, black/African-American ERGs, parenting ERGs, and religious ERGs are some of the many types.

CCDI's guide *Employee Resource Groups: Toolkit for Diversity and Inclusion Practitioners* notes that the purpose of ERGs is to "provide groups of employees with a formal structure within the organization to support their unique needs as they relate to specific personally identifying characteristics, including visible and invisible identities or qualities."[4] An ERG's purpose is completely dependent on the organization. In the public sector, an ERG may focus primarily (if not completely) internally, whereas an ERG in a consulting firm may have both an internal (support and education) and external (business development) mandate. There's no wrong or right way; it's completely dependent on the organization. The US Department of Energy has nine different ERGs: Asian American Pacific Islander Network; Blacks in Government (BIG), Energy Chapter; Community for the Advancement of Latinos at DOE; Disability Employment Task Force, EnergyVets; Federally Employed Women; LGBTQ Employees and Allies; Native American Employees; Professional Opportunities for Women at Energy Realized; and Women's Affinity Group.[5] Most have strictly internally focused mandates, but those with an external focus concentrate on recruiting.

ERGs should not just be social clubs. They need to have a purpose. For example, a midsize private-sector client of mine has a Network for Parents of Children with Special Needs, which is an internal support group. It brings in different speakers to provide education for members and also acts as an informal support body for those in need. Although still on the "social" side of the equation, it's not like it's a group of coworkers getting together over drinks to talk about the latest "sportsball" winning thingy. The mandate benefits the members by giving them a place to turn to during difficult times, and it benefits the organization by increasing the engagement of those in the group.

Another example is one of the first LGBTQ2+ ERGs in Canada, namely, the Gay and Lesbian Organization of Bell Employees, or GLOBE.[6] Much of the work of GLOBE was to lobby Bell Canada to offer domestic-partner benefits to same-sex couples, long before this was legally required. Although ERGs should definitely not be lobbyists, sometimes they have no choice. And the purpose of this ERG went well beyond that and also "participated in fundraising activities, organized social events, and developed an outreach program to further links to similar groups."[7] Bell's LGBTQ2+ group is working on much different projects today, for obvious reasons.

You need a few critical pieces to ensure success with ERGs:

Formalize them. There are varying beliefs about the need for formality with ERGs, but I can tell you—it's critical. ERGs become an "arm" of the organization. They might represent the employer at a recruiting event or in the community. Without some formality, who knows what they could get up to. (Insert ominous organ music here.) Formality does not take away from the work of the group. Far from it. It gives it a framework in which to operate. Formality means having an application process, a mandate and vision, and a plan. This is all the more important if you . . .

Give them a budget. If they don't have any money to spend, what do you expect them to do? I'm not talking six figures, but a few dollars to bring in a speaker or plan an event for the entire organization would be nice. Don't expect them to pay for things themselves, and don't expect them to charge a "membership fee." That's insulting. ERGs provide as much value to the organization as they do to the individuals. All in all, the budget needs to be tied to the next point.

Have objectives and execute. So many ERGs don't have objectives. People think, "We need an ERG for X," and then they have no idea why. I could give you a list of reasons why an ERG would be valuable, but that's not my job, or perhaps yours. The ERG needs to determine what they want to do, how they are going to do it, and what it's going to cost. Then they need to deliver on those objectives and report back to the organization about what they've achieved. Objectives should always benefit the ERG and its members but also the organization overall. That last point is crucial, and it leads back to the first point above and the next one below.

Create alignment. Whatever the objectives are, they need to align with those of the organization. For example, if the ERG decides they want to focus on recruiting, but organizationally you're focused on laying off half your employees, you're out of alignment. The activities of the ERG must be in alignment with the organization overall. And so your ERGs must have some oversight, either by an executive sponsor or your diversity council, or through a reporting relationship to your full- or part-time D&I resources.

Partner. Partnering with other internal groups is important. That might be partnering with an internal resource like IT or marketing and communications, or it might be partnering with another ERG that wants to achieve the same goal. For example, if the ERG's goal is to recruit more people with disabilities into the organization, then they need to work with the talent-attraction team to determine how best to do that. Moreover, if the Indigenous ERG has the same goal, you might as well work together on the project to ensure you maximize efficiencies. Far too often I hear ERGs say, "We really need to focus on X," but they have no idea how to do that. Or worse, they do things without realizing they've just reinvented the wheel.

Include allies. Some people will say you shouldn't include allies in your ERGs. I respectfully disagree. Allies are people who aren't part of the constituency that the ERG aims to serve. Men are allies of women's networks; straight and cisgender people are allies of LGBTQ2+ networks; and so on. Having started an ERG, I can say that one of my biggest regrets was not including allies from the start. I was one of the people who started an LGBTQ2+ ERG at a former employer, and we decided that we should exclude allies. We believed it was the right decision at the time. But the result was that the network became known as a "social club," and allies felt excluded. On top of that, there were LGBTQ2+ people who felt they didn't need to join because they didn't need more friends. Allies can play an important role in the advancement of your ERG's agenda and in moving toward true inclusion overall. The job of allies isn't to "take over" or "save the day." It's to listen and lend support where needed (and asked for).

Recognize them. Lastly, recognize ERGs for the value that they bring to the organization. Too often leadership thinks of ERGs as "those social clubs," like women's networks where members just get together, drink wine, and complain about the menfolk. That happens, right?

Hardly! I've seen many examples of ERGs becoming powerful entities within organizations. A Muslim ERG at one large accounting firm brought in a substantial audit thanks to their relationships within the community. A women's ERG at a large global bank puts on an annual conference that is attended by CEOs and major political players. ERGs deserve respect. And they deserve recognition, which takes two forms. The first is simply noticing and acknowledging the value that an ERG brings to an organization. I encourage you to spend some time with your ERGs and find out about all the good work they've been doing to help make your workplace more inclusive for people. Second, value the time that people put into ERGs. ERGs are volunteer initiatives. Their members already have full-time roles. If a person gives extra time to help run the ERG, recognize them as going above and beyond in their role overall.

Far more information on the leading practices in setting up ERGs can be found in CCDI's free *Employee Resource Groups* toolkit.[8] They key is to understand that they are an important, valuable component of any organization's diversity and inclusion strategy.

Value of D&I Practitioners

I've mentioned D&I practitioners in this book a few times, and I would be remiss if I didn't include a section on the value that they bring to the table.

It's no secret that I advocate for the hiring of full-time, or at the very least part-time, resources with the word "diversity" in their title. The ideal is to have a chief diversity (or inclusion) officer, but I'll accept things like head of diversity; director of diversity and inclusion; or manager of equity, diversity, and inclusion. I don't have some obscene desire for a community of like-minded professionals that all see me as their deity. (Although now that you mention it . . .) I advocate for hiring people to do diversity and inclusion work because *someone needs to do the work*. I cringe when I hear leaders spout off about how important diversity and inclusion is to their organization, and what a strategic priority it is—and yet they have no one actually doing the work. Or it's bolted onto someone else's job title, like manager, HR and diversity; or senior manager, CSR and diversity.

When I started in this profession fifteen years ago, a small handful of people had the word "diversity" in their title, but we were few and far between. Slowly, we've seen that number increase. Why? Because we get stuff done! One organization I worked with had a council that had developed a strategic plan for the year. My team and I were brought in to execute the plan. What they had planned to accomplish in a year, we delivered in three months. Not because we're amazing, but because it was our job. We didn't have anything else to do. We weren't leading a major business unit and doing diversity work off the corner of our desks. As such, we were able to deliver.

This is a "you get what you pay for" situation. If you don't invest any money, meaning you don't have a dedicated resource, you won't get much in return. It's completely inappropriate for employers to expect people to volunteer their time to drive forward a diversity and inclusion agenda when it's supposed to be a "strategic priority" and it's entirely beneficial to the employer.

Any organization with 1,000 to 1,500 employees should have at least one full-time employee dedicated to diversity (and in organizations of more than 2,500 employees, this position should be at an executive level—more on that in the following chapter). Those numbers aren't based on math or a study, but on my fifteen years of experience. You can't just stop at one, either, with the scale of D&I practitioners to employees at approximately one FTE (full-time equivalent) to every 1,000 to 1,500 people. That formula flattens out the larger the workforce gets, and ultimately you need to have a plan to determine how many people you have in D&I and what their roles are. Smaller organizations get a bit of a pass. Less than 1,000 employees and you're fine to have a part-time person who has other responsibilities. Less than 250 and you're good with a volunteer committee or council. We need to be realistic. But any organization with more than 1,000 employees should have one person whose sole job it is to work on D&I in some way, shape, or form.

D&I is a specialty. It takes education and time to become good at the job. More often than I care to mention, people are dropped into D&I roles as a "development opportunity." (I assume they do the same with doctors and lawyers.) I will admit that I was one of those people. My experience was mostly in IT consulting, but I put up my hand to take on the D&I file, and they gave me the job. I suspect they thought if I screwed it up, it wouldn't be a big deal, and I could go back to my "real" job. I just happened to be good at it. That doesn't make it right.

Being a D&I practitioner requires a certain level of skill. It's complicated enough that CCDI developed its own designation—the Canadian Certified Inclusion Professional, or CCIP—that includes an extensive competency framework.[9]

D&I is an unregulated profession. Literally anyone can wake up in the morning and decide they're a D&I professional, regardless of their skills or experience. And it happens, literally, every week. I can't tell you the number of people who reach out to me and describe themselves as D&I practitioners, but their résumés say that last week they were a yoga instructor. (No offence to yoga or yoga instructors.) That said, as more people start to have "diversity" in their job title, the profession is maturing. As organizations hire D&I practitioners, they look to frameworks (like the CCIP) to ensure they get the right people for the job.

And that's where the value comes in. A good D&I professional is a lot of things: an advocate, a realist, a pragmatist, a strategist, an executor, a subject-matter expert, a visionary, and a changemaker. A good D&I professional can help their employer navigate this wacky world that is diversity and inclusion.

D&I is complex. It involves a significant number of moving parts and variables. And it's made more complex by the sheer size of our countries. As Winston Churchill once said, it's "a riddle, wrapped in a mystery, inside an enigma." Admittedly, he was talking about Russia, but it's the same difference. The key to unraveling the "ridmygma" (a combo of Churchill's key words—I'm trying it on and am pretty sure it's going to be a hit) is a good D&I professional—a person that has change management and project management experience, some subject-matter knowledge, and the ability to see the big picture and guide an organization along its journey. Take that, ridmygma!

THE KEY INGREDIENTS 151

Key Takeaways

- Diversity councils are an underutilized resource that can have a significant impact.

- Employee resource groups can be a powerful extension of your organization, if managed properly.

- D&I practitioners are the "doers" of D&I, and you need doers to get things done.

10

FROM THE LEADING EDGE TO THE BLEEDING EDGE

Employers perpetually ask me about "best practices" in D&I: "What's best practice in our industry? What best practices should we be looking at to improve our work?" I never use the term "best practice," because the "best" part troubles me. What's "best" for one employer won't be even close to "best" for another. It might be best for a bank to introduce technology that monitors the daily transactions of its customers, but that might not be best for a gymnasium. I do use the terms "leading practice" or "promising practice."

And now I'm going to contradict myself completely. There *is* a "best" practice in D&I, and it has been completely missed in most organizations: employing a chief diversity officer (CDO).

Canada has very few true chief diversity officers. And by that, I mean that I can think of two who are actually doing the job. To be clear (because I can feel the stink eye coming my way), there are more people with the *title* of chief diversity officer, but they're not *true* CDOs. Not in the true sense. Not as the role is intended. The United States has far more CDOs, but from what I've seen, the positions are mostly about title and not about *authority* and *accountability*, which are the key words here.

In this chapter I break down the responsibilities of a *true* chief diversity officer and why it's critical that employers move to create this position if they want to reach the elusive goal of inclusion. Before we begin, however, a note about size: Most of this content is applicable for organizations of about 2,500 or more employees. Although every organization should name a chief diversity officer at an executive-level position, in organizations smaller than 2,500 employees, it is unrealistic to have a full-time CDO at a senior level. You'll need to adapt.

Executive-Level Position

A true chief diversity officer has an executive-level position. They should hold the second or third highest position within an organization (in other words, ideally reporting to the top person) and be part of the most senior leadership. Some employers in Canada—banks in particular—have CDOs at the vice president or assistant vice president level. That's a start, but let's be honest: VPs at banks are pretty common, and few, if any, are part of the "senior executive." A true CDO has a place at the table just like the CHRO, CFO, COO, CIO, CMO, and any other C-acronym. That's because their job is to provide a D&I lens to everything the organization does, and that includes human resources, finance, operations, information, and marketing.

Reporting and Access

A true CDO reports directly to the most senior person in an organization (CEO, president, executive director, and so on) or, at the very least, to one of that person's direct reports, with a dotted reporting line to the person at the top. That's critical because access is imperative. As I mentioned earlier, and it bears repeating, tone from the top is one of the most important components of a successful D&I journey. A true CDO has direct access to the most senior person to ensure that the highest levels of leadership are championing D&I directly.

Full(ish) Time

As I've said, this is work—a lot of work. Being a true CDO is a full-time job. The job can't be done off the side of their desk— at least, not if the CDO is expected to do the work properly. D&I takes up the entire desk and then some.

Some Canadian employers—consulting, accounting, and law firms, for example—have named high-ranking people as their CDOs, but very few are full-time. Most of these individuals have full-time jobs, and the CDO title is meant to be more "executive sponsor" than anything. So, if you have a CDO 10 percent of the time, you're going to get what you pay for. A true CDO doesn't have another job. D&I *is* their job.

If you *must*, you can pair files, such as D&I and engagement, D&I and culture, or D&I and corporate social responsibility, giving a CDO more than one job. This scenario is not ideal, but it will work, provided that the two areas are interconnected and the CDO has an appropriate team to work with on both files. However, if you've paired D&I and finance or D&I and marketing, you've combined two things that don't go together. You may as well have a person responsible for diversity and national defense.

A Team Leader

A true CDO has a team. If you don't give them a team, they won't be able to get things done. They can't be expected to be strategic and simultaneously execute. Of course, they'll deliver programs and initiatives, but since D&I is intended to layer over an entire organization (which I'll talk about in a minute), CDOs need an appropriate team to deliver on some fairly significant work. However, you don't need to duplicate resources. The CDO may need a "piece" of someone in IT to make the organization's website accessible, and someone in marketing and communications to develop D&I-specific content, and so on, but they don't necessarily need to have their own IT and marketing and communications resources. That said, they still need people to do the work, and you can't *just* rely on people who have other responsibilities.

Plus, just as they need resources, CDOs need budgets. Stuff costs money. You can't expect a CDO to deliver programs and initiatives and not spend some cash. Does your research and development function have a budget? Does human resources have a budget? Do you see where I'm going? CDOs need to spend some money so that they can deliver. If D&I is as big a priority as some organizations *say* it is, then there's a budget that shows it's a priority. And remember— you will see a return on investment that can (and must) be measured! If there's a budget, your CDO will have to prove the impact of their efforts.

So Much More Than People

This is the biggest, most important part of this chapter. Traditionally, D&I has been thought of as an "HR thing." That is what I like to call "mistaken." D&I isn't an HR program, not if it's done right. A true CDO has accountability for so much more than people, holds the big picture, and applies a D&I lens to every aspect of the work and the resources doing it. When done correctly, D&I layers over an organization and everything that organization does, from guaranteeing that marketing materials reflect your customers, to updating facilities and technology so that they're accessible, to developing a diverse supply chain, and beyond.

Marketing and Communications

Marketing and communications should have a prominent role in any organization, and because it's all about how you present your business—both internally and externally—applying a D&I lens to it ensures you're not inadvertently sending the wrong message.

To be blunt, some in marketing and communications are a bit clueless about D&I, particularly those in the advertising world (oh yes, I went there). I often reference the story of a large company (that shall remain nameless) and their advertising campaign to demonstrate how *not* to do D&I. The company, under the not-so-sage guidance of a "cutting-edge" advertising firm, ran a series of ads, and all the people in the ads were white. Some of the company's customers were white, but many weren't.

If said large company had a chief diversity officer, they would have ensured a broader representation in the models, which would have been more reflective of their customer. The campaign would not have been a source of embarrassment, and the company wouldn't have looked out of touch with the consumer.

IT

The most obvious D&I layer with IT is around accessibility. Is your website fully accessible? If you're launching a new app, will it meet WCAG 2.0 standards? Do you even know what WCAG is? (It's the Web Content Accessibility Guidelines, a

set of global standards around accessibility of web content.[1])
What if your company were to hire a person with low vision
who required a screen reader? Would it be compatible with
your systems? A CDO safeguards against barriers to access
for everyone.

Facilities Management

Another obvious area where D&I layers over an organization
is in facilities management, again around accessibility. Are
your facilities completely barrier-free? Building codes across
North America are the bare minimum of what you should be
doing to ensure your facilities are barrier-free.

Beyond accessibility, do you have a prayer or reflection
room on-site? The value of these is that, when employers recognize that we don't all pray the same way, providing prayer
or reflection rooms increases the engagement of the people
who use them. The time saved by people being able to stay
on-site rather than go to a local mosque or temple to pray also
has value. Prayer rooms are becoming commonplace because
D&I people have been making the case to include them. And
what about gender-neutral washrooms? Many aspects of
facilities management should have a D&I lens applied to
them, and a CDO can ensure that's happening.

Procurement and Supply Chain

As I mentioned previously, supplier diversity is a very advanced
topic. Although a critical focus in the United States, supplier

diversity hasn't taken hold in Canada, arguably because we don't have true chief diversity officers driving the work.

In short, supplier diversity is where a company commits a percentage of their annual procurement to buy specifically from businesses that are 51 percent owned and operated by women, people of color, people with disabilities, LGBTQ2+ people, veterans, and Indigenous people. Without going into too much detail (because I've got other books to write), the purpose is to remove barriers and to help stimulate the economy. A CDO takes responsibility for crafting and executing a supplier diversity strategy with the objective of leveraging a company's buying power to provide opportunity to minority-owned businesses.

Products and Services

What does your organization do? What products or services do you offer? And before you think otherwise, every organization offers a product or service. Hospitals provide medical services. Municipalities provide services like garbage collection (and much more). Your "customer" may be a resident, a patient, a consumer, or another company. If you're the City of Toronto, where some 40 percent of residents speak a language other than English or French at home, do you offer your services in another language? If you're a bank, do you have specific products that target LGBTQ2+ consumers, keeping in mind that segment represents nearly $4 trillion in annual spending power?[2]

There's a somewhat famous story about the invention of voice-recognition software. The original versions had trouble recognizing women and people with "foreign" accents (those with something other than English as a first language).[3] Why might that be? Likely because the people who designed the software were men who had English as a first language.

The solution to that problem would've been simple: either have women and people who speak with foreign accents on the team, or test the product with women and people who speak with foreign accents.

Another story has the opposite outcome: Frito-Lay (yes, the chip company) wanted to get into the LatinX/Hispanic market in the United States. It's worth billions, and they recognized they were missing out.[4] They had tried with a few different products, but they'd had little success. Then they turned to their LatinX/Hispanic employee resource group, called Adelante (which is Spanish for "ahead"), leveraging them as a de facto market research group. As Frito-Lay employees, they had a vested interest in the successful launch of a new product. Long story short, thanks to the input of the Adelante members and their family and friends, Frito-Lay launched Doritos Guacamole Tortilla Chips, generating $100 million in sales of that product in the first year—one of the best product launches in the company's history.

The moral of the story is that part of a true CDO's job is to think about the products and services offered and identify opportunities for your organization to either service customers better or offer new products and services that lead to new market segments. Without someone thinking specifically about the opportunities, your organization may be missing out.

A chief diversity officer examines everything your organization does and applies a D&I lens. HR is an important part of that, but as you have just learned, the work goes way beyond resources. Those organizations that install true CDOs will be the ones on the bleeding edge, and they'll leave their competition in the dust. Mic drop!

Key Takeaways

- Companies with a chief diversity officer who has appropriate accountability and authority are at the leading edge of D&I.

- A CDO touches so much more than people—marketing, product development, customers, and so on.

- Allocating CDOs an appropriate team, a budget, and a reporting structure with a direct or dotted line to the most senior person sets them up for success.

WHITE MAN TRUMPS ALL

hesitated to write this chapter. In fact, it's the one that took me the most time to write. I kept coming back to it and then feeling like I was sounding like an arrogant jerk (more so than usual). In the end I decided it's important to include because the conversation around privilege, and more importantly what to do with privilege, doesn't happen enough.

I came out as gay in 1987. At the time, it wasn't such a friendly place for LGBTQ2+ people. Although being LGBTQ2+ was no longer criminalized in Canada, it certainly wasn't celebrated, nor was it safe. *RuPaul's Drag Race*, *Will and Grace*, and *Brokeback Mountain* were all more than a decade away. We were in the (early) days of the HIV/AIDS epidemic, and LGBTQ2+ people, particularly gay men, were seen as villains, receiving our just rewards for our sinful ways. We were the pariah of the country.

Over time, attitudes toward LGBTQ2+ have changed. In 1997, only 41 percent of Canadians were in favor of same-sex marriage, compared to 74 percent in 2017.[1] According to a study conducted by Public Square Research and Maru/Blue for CBC News in May 2019, 85 percent of Canadians identify as being "LGBTQ-friendly,"[2] so it's fair to say the change in attitude has been monumental in a short period of time, relatively speaking.

The caveat here is that the change has taken place for only *some* LGBTQ2+ people—specifically, white cisgender men. There are many LGBTQ2+ people—women, people of color, trans folk—that would say they're still living in an unsafe world. That same study by Public Square Research and Maru/Blue found that 65 percent of all Canadians said they agreed with the statement "we have gone too far in accommodating every group in society," and 24 percent said that too many immigrants come from visible minorities.[3] Life is rosy—just not for everyone.

As a society, we tend to think of all LGBTQ2+ people as a group. We're presented as one big community, which is entirely inaccurate. In fact, we're a series of communities that have been strung together by one acronym. Gays are different from lesbians (gay is generally used by men, lesbian by women). Two-spirit people have a very different lived experience than bisexuals, particularly white bi people. Some of the letters in the abbreviation are sexual orientations; some are gender-related; some are both. There's a trend of older LGBTQ2+ folks, as they move into retirements homes and seniors' residences, going back into the closet for their own protection; this is happening at a time when we had the first gay man running to be president of the United States. It's simplistic to think that we're all having the same glorious, rainbow-filled experience in life.

At a May 2019 conference in Yellowknife, Northwest Territories, I had the distinct pleasure of giving a keynote speech to the Association of Workers Compensation Boards of Canada. During my downtime, I socialized with a group of conference participants, with whom I had dinner one evening. Over our meal, the conversation led to the progress made toward the inclusion of LGBTQ2+ peoples, with one diner noting how included I was among this entirely straight, entirely white, mostly male group. So, he wondered, what was the issue? Why did we still need to protest and celebrate?

I corrected him with the phrase "white man trumps all." He looked at me, puzzled. I explained that yes, I'm included. But I'm a cisgender white man. A group of white men look at me but don't see "gay" first; they see "white man" first. Gay is second, and a distant second at that. They don't care that I'm gay, because the fact that I'm a white man allows them to feel like they're among their own. I don't make them uncomfortable anymore.

Since blurting this out at dinner, I've considered what I meant more deeply. (This is how most of my great thoughts occur: speak first, think later.) When I came out of the closet, openly gay people being verbally and physically assaulted on the street was common. The Pride "celebration" was a protest in the truest sense. We were fighting for our lives. Fast-forward thirty years and the prime minister of Canada is marching in Pride parades and has an LGBTQ2+ advisor.[4] President Trump ... not so much. We've come a long way, but please don't call me "baby."

However, other communities haven't made the same progress in anywhere near as short a period. The broad Civil Rights movement began in the late 1800s. In Canada, white and black women did not receive the right to vote until 1918. In the United States, that didn't happen until 1920, and in some Southern states, African-American women were unable to freely exercise their right to vote up until the 1960s (and arguably, little has changed). Women in the province of Quebec did not receive full, equal rights until 1944.[5] Asian people were not granted equal rights until after World War II, in 1949. Inuit people were not granted equal rights until 1950, and it was not until 1960 that equal rights were extended to First Nations people without requiring them to give up their treaty status.[6] I could go on ... and on ... and on. And these are just legislative rights. Cultural and societal acceptance has taken a significantly longer time, if it has occurred at all. Can we get a little justice for Trayvon Martin?

In 2019, women made somewhere between $0.69 to $0.87 for every dollar made by a man.[7] The numbers are worse for Indigenous women, women of color, and newcomer women. You only have to do a quick media scan of any *reputable* media source to find stories of racism, ableism, transphobia, anti-Islamic sentiment, and so on.

Yet, Pete Buttigieg ran to become the Democratic candidate for president of the United States. Pete is a veteran who served two tours in Afghanistan and is a Rhodes scholar; he speaks eight languages, and he is the very popular mayor of South Bend, Indiana. He's also gay. And no one really cares. No one spoke about his sexual orientation. It didn't come up in a negative way in any story from any reputable news outlet. In fact, most of the Democratic candidates were fighting to be the most LGBTQ2+ friendly (did you see Kamala Harris's jacket at LA Pride?). People were trying to out-gay the gay guy. The biggest "negative" news story about Mayor Pete was how difficult it is to pronounce his name (Buddha-judge is my favorite phonetical pronunciation) and that he didn't resonate with African-American voters. But he's white. And that trumps all (little *t*, not big *T*).

Kamala Harris was also a front-runner to be the Democratic candidate, but she didn't even make the Iowa primary. She is a woman of color, her father being black and her mother South Asian. She has an equally impressive résumé—she's a lawyer, she graduated from Harvard, and she served as the district attorney for San Francisco from 2004 to 2011 and the attorney general of California from 2011 to 2017. She was elected as a US senator in 2017, and she ran to be president. Yet debate about how black she is swirled around her. During the first debate among the Democratic candidates, Donald Trump Jr. retweeted to his millions of followers the message: "Kamala Harris is *not* an American Black. She is half Indian and half Jamaican."[8] The original tweet came from someone who identifies as African American, but little Donny didn't retweet it because he agrees. He retweeted it because race-baiting appeals to his daddy's base.

My point is that two equally qualified candidates were spoken of in disparate ways: one positively and one for not being black enough. In the Oppression Olympics, being gay is far better than being black.[9] But if Mayor Pete were black *and* gay... oh boy.

People talk about the Oppression Olympics as if it's mythical, but it isn't. It's real. LGBTQ2+ folks who are white and cisgender skipped past people of color on the road to full inclusion. In this case, high tide has not raised all boats. And that's a problem.

White man trumps all.

White Guilt versus White Privilege

Dictionary.com defines white guilt as "the feelings of shame and remorse some white people experience when they recognize the legacy of racism and racial injustice and perceive the ways they have benefited from it."[10] The concept of white guilt isn't new. It dates back as far as 1978 and an anti-racism trainer named Judith H. Katz, who published a book called *White Awareness: Handbook for Anti-Racism Training*. She has been critical of what she called self-indulgent white-guilt fixations.[11] Sounds like fun!

It seems strange to me that in my long career in D&I, the first time white guilt came up was in 2019, when I was delivering training for a large financial services organization.

In one session, a participant (who I thought was completely disengaged, but apparently, he was listening intently, which just goes to show...) said that he felt guilty for being white. I was surprised to hear it and thanked him for his openness. I then asked how many others felt guilty for being white. I was stunned to see a good third of people in the room put up their hands. I've since been asking this question in training sessions and continue to see a large number of hands raised. I'm clearly onto something. But what to do about it?

It never dawned on me to feel guilty about the color of my skin, just as it never crossed my mind to consider another person as less-than because of the color of theirs. Don't get me wrong; I'm not perfect—I've got more issues than *National Geographic*. I just don't think of the color of a person's skin as a determinant of anything. My response to the man who had expressed his guilt, and to all those subsequently, has been somewhat simple: guilt is a useless emotion... what are you going to do about it?

Shantideva, an eighth-century Indian Buddhist sage, once said, "If you can solve your problem, then what is the need of worrying? If you can't solve it, then what is the use of worrying?" Give it up for Shantideva! All kidding aside (don't worry, I'm still going to kid), guilt serves no purpose. Feeling guilty about something doesn't benefit the person who has been wronged, and it certainly doesn't benefit the person who is feeling guilty.

Guilt may be a useless emotion, but it does lead to a conversation about privilege. As I asked this particular man, "How are you going to use your privilege to the benefit of others?"

As a refresher, "privilege" is "a special right, advantage, or immunity granted or available only to a particular person or group of people."[12] Keeping in mind that race is a social construct (in other words, it's socially "agreed upon" but doesn't exist in objective reality—the concept of "race" is not reflective of biology),[13] people of Caucasian background have a great deal of privilege. White men have even more privilege. Even I, as a gay man who lives with a disability, am still a white man. That privilege means that I've never been stopped by the police because they suspected I might have stolen the car I was driving. No one has ever assumed I wasn't born in Canada. No one has ever said to me, "Oh, I didn't think you'd be white."

Privilege isn't a good or bad thing. It just is. It exists, and there is literally nothing you can do to get rid of or get it. Well, let me qualify that: To some extent, privilege will always exist, but it will change. It will morph. Look at my sexual orientation. At one point, it was definitely not an advantage. Today...

So, if you've got the white guilt, the solution to relieve your guilt, it would seem to me, is to use your privilege to the advantage of others. It's that simple. Here are a few examples of how you can do just that:

Sponsor someone who doesn't look like you. I'm being a bit cheeky here, but the point is to sponsor someone who does not benefit from the same form of privilege as you do. Being a mentor and being a sponsor often get confused. Mentors talk *to* you; sponsors talk *about* you. Being a sponsor means you take responsibility for someone's career advancement. It becomes your job to identify opportunities to help that person advance their career, and then make sure that people at leadership tables know who that person is. You don't have to be an executive to be a sponsor. You can sponsor someone who's just one level below you.

Become an executive sponsor. Different from individual sponsorship, becoming the executive sponsor of an employee resource group or committee is a great way to use your privilege to the advantage of others. Senior leaders can do this to lend credibility to an ERG or committee doing D&I work. If I say it's important to be inclusive of LGBTQ2+ peoples, it's not going to have the same impact as if a member of the senior leadership team says it. And you don't have to identify as a member of the community. I think the best executive sponsor for a women's ERG or initiative is a man. A lot of power comes with being a SWAM, and sponsoring a women's ERG says, "This is important." The SWAM isn't the savior, but he sends a signal by being in the room. That's using privilege for the advantage of others.

Create space for others. Have you ever been in a meeting where a woman says something and people ignore her, and then a man says the same thing and suddenly people think he's just reinvented the wheel? Every woman reading this is nodding right now. And most men are confused. Well, boys, it happens. A lot. And not just to women.

You can use your privilege to change that. So, when the woman (or newcomer, and so on) says what she says and the man repeats it, it's your job to point out that the woman said it first and people should pay attention. It's your job to use your privilege to ensure everyone has an opportunity to share their ideas.

Get involved, even if it's not about you. You don't have to be black to be part of the black ERG, or a woman to be part of a women's program. Getting involved makes you an ally. Your help can go a long way toward getting things done. Who cares what your motivation is? Just get involved. Attend an event, participate in a discussion, whatever. It's important that allies don't try to ride in and save the day. This isn't about you. Don't try to make it about you. You've had your moment! Show up and ask how you can help.

Listen and encourage others to listen. There's an old saying, "Nothing about us without us," which was originally invoked in Poland in 1505, during the transfer of power from the monarchy to the parliament. In essence, it represents the concept that no policy should be decided without participation of members of the group(s) affected by that policy. Another version is "Nothing for us without us." The expression has been used by many groups over the years, including disability advocates, ethnocultural groups, and Indigenous groups.

Using your privilege to the advantage of others is about doing the work with them, not for them. It's about getting behind a movement. However, the most important thing you can do is listen. Listen to what people have to say. Learn about the experiences of others. Ask questions, specifically things like, "What can I do to help?" Resist your urge to ride in on your steed and save the damsel in distress.

A Note for the Naysayers

As I write this chapter, I can just feel someone (from an under-represented group) thinking, "We don't need your help, white man. We can do it on our own!"

Sorry, folks. That's just not accurate. We can't do it alone. Doing it alone hearkens back to the social justice approach to diversity and inclusion. We've been trying to do it on our own for decades, and we've made so little progress that it's barely recognizable. I believe that one of the reasons LGBTQ2+ inclusion has come as far as it has in such a short period of time is that we engaged our allies. My (straight) parents as an example: they have been fighting for LGBTQ2+ inclusion almost as hard as I have.

We need our allies. We need people like white men, who can walk into a room and say things that we can't. It's the only way we're going to see progress.

Key Takeaways

- Privilege is not something that can be taken or received. It's assigned to you, whether you like it or not.

- There are a significant number of different types of privilege, and you don't have to be a white man to have privilege.

- The only solution is to use your privilege to the advantage of others who don't share the same privilege you have.

12

OVERCOMING
DIVERSITY FATIGUE

My friends at the *Oxford Dictionary* define the word "fatigue" as "extreme tiredness resulting from mental or physical exertion or illness."[1] If you add "diversity" to the beginning of that, it sums up "diversity fatigue" quite well. It's about the exhaustion that comes from the mental or physical efforts related to diversity and inclusion work.

D&I work is a bit thankless, and often its practitioners feel isolated and like they're the only ones who care about the work. Plus, they constantly deal with resistance. All in all, it's exhausting work. The National Health Service in the United Kingdom has a list of tips to fight tiredness:

- Eat often to beat tiredness.
- Get moving [exercise].
- Lose weight to gain energy [if you're overweight].

- Sleep well.
- Reduce stress to boost energy.
- Try talk therapy to beat fatigue.
- Cut out caffeine.
- Drink less alcohol.
- Drink more water for better energy.[2]

Take note, because although this may seem like a strange reference to include, it's going to come in handy as you develop strategies to stay well rested.

There are two types of diversity fatigue: individual and organizational. The source of both may be the same, but the results are quite different for each. Let's look at each of them and see what we can do to overcome them.

Individual Diversity Fatigue

Like I said, this work can be brutal on a D&I practitioner. It's a thankless job. The progress is often painfully slow, and it's hard to remember to stop and celebrate the wins (no matter how small they are), because if you don't, no one will. If you aren't passionate about this work, staying in the field will be difficult. D&I work is where my personal and professional lives met and married. The problem is, diversity fatigue can lead to divorce if you're not careful. You care so much about the work that you end up sacrificing other aspects of your life. Not a good scenario. But there are ways to combat it.

Take care of you, physically. The list above from the NHS is all about taking care of your mental and physical well-being. Go to the gym, go for a walk—whatever you like to do to get moving is what you should do. I'm less concerned about you being a health fanatic and more concerned about you engaging your brain in a different manner. Endorphins are a natural pain and stress reliever, and while there are several ways to produce endorphins, exercise is one of them.[3] So is sex. You pick.

Take care of you, mentally. Being a D&I practitioner is an emotional job. A lot of people in D&I have a deep emotional connection to the work, and as such, taking care of yourself mentally is mandatory. Do talk therapy or speak with a religious leader or spiritual guide. Meditate or do yoga. Whatever you need to do to take care of your mental health, do it. You're going to need all your faculties to overcome fatigue.

Set boundaries. As a D&I practitioner, you must define very strong boundaries and live by them. I've seen way too many people digging themselves out of bad situations because they didn't set boundaries. This tends to be very personal work. But it's also a job. You don't have to attend every event. You can't help every individual just because you care. Know that you *can* and *should* leave the job at the office and disconnect at night and on weekends. I promise the work will still be there when you get back.

Rely on your network. One of the best things I have as a D&I practitioner is my network. When I started doing this work,

I was the only person in my organization, and I felt pretty alone. I cobbled together a group of peers from other organizations whom I could rely on. This informal network of people would get together and talk about the work we were doing. The group became very close, and we're still quite tight. I always knew that if I had a challenge, I could pick up the phone and someone would be able to share some words of encouragement that would recharge my battery. Do as I did. Find a group of peers from other organizations and create a network that you can rely on in your times of need, or just when you need an ear.

Know you're only human. Human beings are not machines. We cannot work eight-plus hours a day without breaks and expect to function properly. Working when you work best (I'm a morning person), taking regular coffee and lunch breaks, and above all, *taking your vacation time*, are imperative.

The best thing you can do for yourself and your employer is to recharge so that you can look at the challenges with fresh eyes, as opposed to through the fog of exhaustion.

Organizational Diversity Fatigue

Organizational diversity fatigue affects the majority of an organization. The fatigue stems from a few sources. One of the most common reasons for diversity fatigue is lack of progress. Progress with this work is often very slow, and as such, it's hard to see when you've improved. For example, diversifying a leadership team can take years, because leadership turnover is notoriously low in most organizations. If you constantly look for the change to occur, it can start to feel like you're never going to make progress.

It can be very hard to cut through the noise of an organization's thousands of projects and initiatives, not the least of which is D&I. If people don't see your work, they'll start to feel like nothing is happening. Worse is when competing priorities become conflicting priorities—for example, when organizations diversifying their workforce suddenly have to go through a downsizing or rightsizing exercise, and they use the "last in, first out" methodology to decide who will stay and who will go. If the majority of your diversity is recent, they'll also be the first to go.

As we discussed above, the people who do this work are passionate about it. And as the saying goes, the flame that burns twice as bright burns half as long. Far too often, good work falls apart because only one or a few people do it, and they burn out, usually when they're not being recognized for the value D&I brings to the organization.

I often describe diversity and inclusion work like driving a car uphill, continuously. If you put your foot on the brakes, you stop moving. If you take your foot off the gas, you will roll backward. You will never get to a flat spot where you can coast, or to a point where you're rolling downhill. That's just not how this works. You can't take your foot off the gas. Ever. But a few simple yet quite effective strategies will combat organizational fatigue:

Make noise. The best way to compete with all the other organizational priorities and cut through so people see what you're doing is to make noise, often. Don't wait for a huge announcement. Communicate consistently and frequently. At least once a month, send out a message about diversity and inclusion. It can be simple: an e-mail about an upcoming event; a note in the organization newsletter about an ERG initiative; a blog post about D&I from your most senior leader. Work with your communications team to develop an annual communications calendar, so you know what message you're going to push out every month and by what vehicle. Plan it in advance so you're not scrambling to figure out your message. Change it up, so it's a new topic every month. Keeping D&I front and center consistently will remind people that you're at work, even if they can't see significant change.

Go old-school. One of the best communications vehicles has become good old-fashioned paper. As an environmentalist, I hesitate to include this, but considering how far away from paper we've gone, when a poster appears on a wall or a postcard appears on your desk, it catches your attention, and people read it. Limit this to once or twice a year and it will have a big impact. Use paper to promote a big message.

Goldilocks that shizzle. When you're developing your strategy, size your initiatives appropriately. If all the projects are "small" (meaning you can do them in less than a year), then your D&I work will come across as lip service. If all your projects are "large" (meaning you will need more than three years to see results), then you're not going to be perceived as making progress. Get it "just right," with initiatives that are small, medium, and large. The small projects will support your communications, giving you something to talk about. The medium projects will have more impact, and although they will take longer to bear fruit (one to two years), they'll also be seen as more substantive than the small ones. When you deliver the large projects, they will come across as really influential.

Recognize the work. Consider creating a monthly or quarterly Leadership Award for Diversity and Inclusion. That way your most senior leader can recognize the people who are doing the work on a regular basis, which will provide a boost of energy to the people already involved and encourage more people to engage in the change.

Share the load. Sharing the load is imperative. Involve people, be it with committees or ERGs, to make sure that more than one person does the work. With many people doing the work, you reduce the chances of initiatives falling apart.

Celebrate the wins. D&I practitioners are terrible about patting themselves on the back, but you have to celebrate your wins, no matter how small they are, so that people perceive the progress that is happening. Even if you feel it's a small win, have a little celebration. Do something to recognize that the organization's hard work is paying off.

Seek to win awards. Many people question the value of awards, but they can be beneficial. One research study found that more than 600 quality corporate award winners had 37 per-cent more sales growth and 44 percent higher stock price return than their peers.[4] If nothing else, winning an award sends a message to your employees that the organization is doing something right. You're being recognized publicly. That can positively affect organizational pride. It also sends a mes-sage to potential talent and customers that you're focused on D&I—and for those who care, that will matter. If you win an award, shout it from the rooftops. Issue a press release; blast social media; use the award logo on your website and e-mail signature; and otherwise do everything you can to celebrate that you've been recognized.

Key Takeaways

- Diversity fatigue is real, and it affects both the individual D&I practitioners and champions *and* the organization.

- As individuals and as an organization, stop and celebrate your accomplishments so that you don't let the fatigue win.

- Every win is worth celebrating.

WHAT GETS IN THE WAY?

Since taking on this work full-time, I've spent many hours examining what gets in the way of D&I, and thinking about why inclusion doesn't "just happen." But I've always found it confusing. Aren't we all trying to "do the right thing"? I was raised in a left-leaning household. My parents were hippies. I was taught that it was my responsibility to be inclusive of others. Wasn't everyone?

Many things can and do get in the way of successful diversity and inclusion: lack of resources; lack of leadership buy-in; competing priorities; alien invasion (one of those doesn't really get in the way so much as destroy life on the planet). But even when all the pieces are in place, failure still happens where we should see success. And I think I've come up with the answer to why that is: self-interest.

Oxford defines self-interest as "one's personal interest or advantage, especially when pursued without regard for others."[1] You've seen examples, such as the person who speeds past you in the right lane, expecting you to let them in, even though they could clearly see the lane was coming to an end. They just wanted to get one car-length ahead. You've surely observed people at the airport milling around the gate even though they can see the lines of people queueing up. When their zone gets called, they push their way in—ahead of all the people who had patiently waited—as if they'll get to the destination ahead of everyone else.

Everyone has self-interest in some way. Even the most selfless people have their own agenda. Take Mahatma Gandhi. He was pretty selfless, right? He was an activist who protested British rule of India in the early 1900s. That's pretty selfless. But is it? Didn't he gain when India returned to independence? Okay, that example is a little extreme, and I can feel I'm losing my audience. I'm a big Gandhi fan. He did some great work. #GoGandhi. An independent India was a good idea. I'm completely on board with decolonization of the world. But my point is that even those we perceive to be the most selfless have a cause or agenda.

The first time I considered self-interest as a concept in diversity and inclusion was when I was working for an organization with a new CEO and his whole schtick was "we need to get rid of self-interest" as part of his "company first" manifesto. Great intention. Good in theory. Not so good in execution. Smart, well-intentioned people sabotaged the new strategy because they simply couldn't move past their self-interest. From there I started to extrapolate the influence of self-interest on the diversity and inclusion agenda.

Individual Self-Interest

As individuals, most people (although we will let Gandhi off the hook here) have self-interest. People put themselves first. Evidence of that can be seen in a 2019 CBC poll that found that two-thirds of Canadians consider fighting climate change a top priority, but half of Canadians won't spend more than $100 of their own money to address the situation.[2] This is not a D&I example, but it shows how self-interested people can be even when they care deeply about an issue.

Self-interest from a D&I perspective is when you put your own agenda above everyone else's, leading to infighting where there should be harmony. For instance, if a person of color gets a promotion over a white person and the white person drops the accusation that it's a "diversity promotion," that's self-interest through a D&I lens. Could it be that the other person deserved it more? What would the white person say if they lost out to another white person? I could provide a multitude of examples, but more important is to recognize the challenge: most of us operate from a place of self-interest on a daily basis. Doing so makes it very hard to help others if there isn't anything in it for you.

Community Self-Interest

Community self-interest is driven by the individual, but it's when a person puts the self-interest of one group over another. This happens when we care so much about our own community that we prioritize our agenda over any other community, at all costs. Let me use another somewhat controversial example: In 2016, members of the group Black Lives Matter stopped Toronto's Pride parade by conducting a sit-in in the middle of the parade to protest the treatment of marginalized people within the LGBTQ2+ communities. The group were the honored guests, and they held the whole parade hostage until the executive director agreed to a list of demands.

There was a huge outcry, and lines were drawn in the community. Personally, I thought everyone was wrong in this situation. Pride Toronto, at the time, had a long history of appealing to the group with the most money (white, cisgender LGBTQ2+ folks), and they needed to be called out; Black Lives Matter could've done so much more to fix the problem than just go for the media attention; and the Toronto Police ... well, let's just say there are some issues there.

I supported Black Lives Matter up until the list of demands came out. The situation was set up so that the executive director would sign whatever they put in front of him at that moment, but would he have any intention of honoring those demands? You can't put a gun to someone's head and then expect that they will respect you. Yet I was horrified by the reaction of some people—people I respect—who objected to having their parade disrupted. Poor babies ... did you miss your brunch reservation? Insert angry-face emoji.

Black Lives Matter was right, however, to use their moment in the spotlight to draw attention to a gaping hole in the inclusiveness of Pride Toronto. Pride is political. Always has been and likely always will be. But their actions showed community self-interest because they prioritized the self-interest of the black LGBTQ2+ community (as well as the Indigenous and trans communities that they purported to speak for) over the rest of the LGBTQ2+ community. Regardless of why, it still shows a level of self-interest.

Sometimes community self-interest is required, particularly when a community is being ignored. However, if every community could put its self-interest aside and work together, provided each community has a willingness to understand the issues faced by the other, we'd be far further along.

Organizational Self-Interest

Organizational self-interest happens when an organization—in this case an employer—puts the organization's interest above that of others, such as the community served. The most immediate example that comes to mind is Quebec's passing of Bill 21, the so-called Secularism Law. The actual name of the act is "An Act respecting the laicity of the State." For readers who are not familiar with this delightful piece of legislation, it makes it illegal for people in positions of authority in public-sector organizations (police officers, teachers, judges, and so on) to wear religious symbols of any kind. And by "any" religious symbol, what we're really talking about is that of Muslim women and members of other "visible" religious minorities. The name of the bill itself is steeped in self-interest. If you break it down, it translates to "an act respecting the principals of the people of the state" (being the Province of Quebec). Aren't religious minorities people of the state?

In this example, the organization (the Coalition Avenir Québec government) has prioritized its self-interest (and the self-interest of the people who voted for them) over the human rights of some of the citizens of the province. If you don't believe me, take note that they included the not-withstanding clause in the legislation. This gives Canadian jurisdictions the ability to opt out of the Canadian Constitution's Charter of Rights and Freedoms for five years.[3] If they thought the act was respectful of people's human rights, why would they include such a clause? If there was no self-interest involved, the act would never have been tabled.

Another readily seen example of organizational self-interest specific to employers is of oil and gas companies that appear to be working with Indigenous communities, but in the end, they are doing what they want, regardless of whether the community supports it.

Self-Interest Is Always Personal

Self-interest is always about the individual. Each example above comes back to the individual. Perhaps the self-interest is "right" and "just," and in the benefit of others, but it's still self-interest. Perhaps the self-interest is in your job description (the role of the CEO of an oil and gas company is to maximize return on investment for shareholders), but that doesn't make it right. And therein lies the rub. We will always live in a world with self-interest. The challenge is to keep self-interest from getting in the way of diversity and inclusion.

I'm not sure I have the perfect solution to that. Or at least I don't have an easy solution for it. Stay with me, because I'm going to get a bit philosophical, but we'll get there. The real solution is to work hard to put aside our self-interest and prioritize the self-interest of others, understanding that we live in a very delicate ecosystem, where our actions may affect someone else. It's the butterfly effect. For those of you who aren't familiar with it, the butterfly effect is the theory that a small change can lead to vastly different outcomes. The concept is usually described as a butterfly flapping its wings, ultimately causing a typhoon.

Consider this: If someone drops a plastic cup on the beach, does that really impact anyone else, or is it a victimless crime? Well, ultimately someone has to pick up the cup and put it in the recycling bin, so no, it's not victimless. It's not as if the cup is going to break down on the beach and magically return to Mother Earth. But what if a seagull picks up the plastic instead, because they like the sweetness of the drink that was in it? And what if that bird drops it in the water? And what if that water takes the cup far out into the lake or ocean? And what if fish start to eat the cup as it breaks down in the water? And what if those fish are caught and become someone's dinner? Now we have someone or a group of "someones" eating fish that may be tainted with plastic. Studies have shown that all plastics may leach chemicals if they're scratched or heated, and these chemicals may cause cancer in humans.[4] Because our friendly neighborhood litterbug didn't take the time to dispose of their plastic cup on the beach, people might get cancer. That may seem like a stretch, but it could, and likely does, happen.

We need to consider the impact of our actions on others. We don't live in isolation—at least, most of us don't. Even a person who lives completely in isolation could do something that might affect others and never be aware of it. The only solution to self-interest is to think. Think long and hard about what you're trying to achieve and then determine if someone else might be hurt or benefited by your actions. You can guess the outcome I'd like you to choose.

Key Takeaways

- Self-interest is usually at the root of failure when D&I doesn't work.

- Individual, community, and organizational self-interest all influence D&I work.

- To be successful in D&I, self-interest needs to be put aside, and there must be a willingness to understand one another's needs in order for us all to move forward as one.

ACKNOWLEDGMENTS

I've learned it's customary to include a list of acknowledgments in a book. This should apparently be a list of people who have helped in the work, and not just the brands of wine you drank while writing it. The more you know...

Let's start with the obvious ones: my family. I am blessed to have a supportive and loving family who have taught me some incredibly important lessons. If it weren't for them, I wouldn't be the person I am today. Because I wouldn't have been born.

Next: My colleagues at CCDI. I'm not going to list them all because there are too many of them, but they're all fantastic! I have said it before, and I'll say it again: I have the pleasure of working beside the most amazing group of thirty-plus people who bought into a vision that I created and have helped make it possible. I learn something every day because I have the chance to work side by side with such smart, capable, visionary people. It makes going to work an absolute pleasure.

There is a long list of people in the D&I space that I regularly call on for advice, guidance, or just to meet for a glass of wine. Many of them are my colleagues now (Deanna, Zakeana, Susan, Anne-Marie), but for those who are not (yet) working for CCDI—rather than me going through a laundry list of names—just understand that I am blessed to know so many great people in this field.

Then we have my dear friend Kate Broer. Kate has been a comrade in arms on the D&I journey since 2007, when she was working at what was then Fraser Milner Casgrain, and I was at KPMG. Many, many times we supported each other through wild and wacky situations, and I'm so pleased to be able to call her a friend.

I'd be remiss if I didn't acknowledge Beth Wilson and Mary Lou Maher of KPMG (Beth formerly, Mary Lou currently). It's because of these two visionary women that I'm working in D&I. They saw something in me, and they set me on my path. So, you have them to blame, and I have them to thank. I also want to recognize Bill MacKinnon, who was the CEO of KPMG when I took on my role. Bill wasn't my CEO for long enough, but when he was, he had my back. He may not have understood everything I was trying to do, but you could never ask for a better champion in your corner.

Last and not least, my husband, Mike. I spent a lot of time wandering around before I bumped into the man who would become my husband. I kissed a lot of frogs. I'm just lucky that one of them turned out to be a prince.

NOTES

This book contains a lot of references. Man, I was busy! To make things easier for you to access these links, we have created an online repository of all the links below. You can find it at **www.michaelbach.com**. You're welcome.

Chapter 1: D&I Defined

1   *Oxford Dictionary*, s.v. "representation (*n.*)," accessed February 13, 2020, https://www.lexico.com/en/definition/representation.

2   *Oxford Dictionary*, s.v. "diversity (*n.*)," accessed February 13, 2020, https://www.lexico.com/en/definition/diversity.

3   Marilyn Loden and Judy Rosener, *Workforce America! Managing Employee Diversity as a Vital Resource* (New York: McGraw-Hill, 1990); Marilyn Loden, *Implementing Diversity* (New York: McGraw-Hill, 1995); Lee Gardenswartz and Anita Rowe, *Diverse Teams at Work: Capitalizing on the Power of Diversity*, 2nd edition (Alexandria, VA: Society for Human Resource Management, 2003).

4   Andrés Tapias, *The Inclusion Paradox: The Post Obama Era and the Transformation of Global Diversity* (Lincolnshire, IL: Hewitt Associates, 2009).

5   Steve L. Robbins quoted in IC Staff, "A Campus Tipping Point and an Opportunity for Understanding Together," Ithaca College, Diversity and Inclusion at IC, July 12, 2016, https://www.ithaca.edu/diversity/news/understanding-together-41871/.

6   "Your Human Rights," United Nations Office of the High Commissioner on Human Rights, accessed February 13, 2020, https://www.ohchr.org/EN/Issues/Pages/WhatareHumanRights.aspx.

7   *Oxford Dictionary*, s.v. "equity (*n.*)," accessed February 13, 2020, https://www.lexico.com/en/definition/equity.

8   Dr. Naheed Dosani (@NaheedD), "#Equality is giving everyone a shoe. #Equity is giving everyone a shoe that fits," Twitter, April 23, 2014, 6:23 p.m., https://twitter.com/naheedd/status/451847459242012672?lang=en.

9   *Oxford Dictionary*, s.v. "accessibility (*n.*)," accessed February 13, 2020, https://www.lexico.com/en/definition/accessibility.

10   *Oxford Dictionary*, s.v. "accommodation (*n.*)," accessed February 13, 2020, https://www.lexico.com/en/definition/accommodation.

11   Kimberlé Crenshaw, "Demarginalizing the Intersection of Race and Sex: A Black Feminist Critique of Antidiscrimination Doctrine, Feminist Theory and Antiracist Politics," The University of Chicago Legal Forum (1989), https://philpapers.org/archive/CREDTI.pdf.

12   Joanna Simpson, *Everyone Belongs: A Toolkit for Applying Intersectionality*, Canadian Research Institute for the Advancement of Women, 2009.

13   United Nations, "Committee on the Elimination of Racial Discrimination, seventieth session," (summary record of the 1791st meeting, Palais Wilson, Geneva, February 21, 2007).

14   Statistics Canada, "Visible Minority Immigrant," accessed February 13, 2020, https://www150.statcan.gc.ca/n1/pub/81-004-x/def/4068739-eng.htm.

15 Michael Bach, "Diversity and the Straight White Able-bodied Man: Putting the Inclusion in Diversity and Inclusion" (presentation, 2008 Conference Board of Canada's Workplace Diversity and Inclusiveness Forum, Toronto, Ontario, January 7, 2009).

16 "How Straight, White, Able-Bodied Men Can Have a Role In Workplace Diversity," CBC Radio, Out in the Open, October 26, 2018, https://www.cbc.ca/radio/outintheopen/allies-1.4850186/how-straight-white-able-bodied-men-can-have-a-role-in-workplace-diversity-1.4850194.

17 Sam Killermann, "Comprehensive* List of LGBTQ+ Vocabulary Definitions," It's Pronounced Metrosexual, December 8, 2017, http://itspronouncedmetrosexual.com/2013/01/a-comprehensive-list-of-lgbtq-term-definitions/.

18 Sam Killermann, "The Genderbread Person Version 3," It's Pronounced Metrosexual, March 16, 2015, http://itspronouncedmetrosexual.com/2015/03/the-genderbread-person-v3/.

19 *Oxford Dictionary*, s.v. "reverse discrimination (*n.*)," accessed February 13, 2020, https://www.lexico.com/en/definition/reverse_discrimination.

20 "Bhinder v. CN, [1985] 2 S.C.R. 561," Judgements of the Supreme Court of Canada, accessed February 13, 2020, https://web.archive.org/web/20071013132621/http://scc.lexum.umontreal.ca/en/1985/1985rcs2-561/1985rcs2-561.html.

21 "Central Alberta Dairy Pool v. Alberta (Human Rights Commission), [1990] 2 S.C.R. 489," Judgements of the Supreme Court of Canada, accessed February 13, 2020, https://web.archive.org/web/20101018050232/http://scc.lexum.umontreal.ca/en/1990/1990scr2-489/1990scr2-489.html.

22 *Oxford Dictionary*, s.v. "privilege (*n.*)," accessed February 13, 2020, https://www.lexico.com/en/definition/privilege.

23 "Number of Mass Shootings in the United States between 1982 and February 2018, by Mass Shooter's Race and Ethnicity," Statista, accessed March 29, 2020, https://www.statista.com/statistics/476456/mass-shootings-in-the-us-by-shooter-s-race/.

Chapter 2: The Models of Diversity and Inclusion

1 *Oxford Dictionary*, s.v. "social justice (*n.*)," accessed February 13, 2020, https://www.lexico.com/en/definition/social_justice.

2 Jesse Gillispie, "Using a Social Justice Framework to Guide Diversity, Equity, and Inclusion Work," National Association of Independent Schools, Fall 2018, https://www.nais.org/magazine/independent-school/fall-2018/using-a-social-justice-framework-to-guide-diversity,-equity,-and-inclusion-work/.

3 *Oxford Dictionary*, s.v. "racist (*adj.*)," accessed February 13, 2020, https://www.lexico.com/en/definition/racist.

4 Vernon Turner, "Executive Summary: Data Growth, Business Opportunities, and the IT Imperatives," The Digital Universe of Opportunities, April 2014, https://www.emc.com/leadership/digital-universe/2014iview/executive-summary.htm.

5 Korn Ferry, "Future of Work: The Global Talent Crunch," 2018, https://dsqapj1lakrkc.cloudfront.net/media/sidebar_downloads/FOWTalentCrunchFinal_Spring2018.pdf.

Chapter 3: The Business Case

1 John Elflein, "Distribution of Nurses in Canada from 2006 to 2016, Gender," August 9, 2019, https://www.statista.com/statistics/496975/nurse-distribution-in-canada-by-gender/.

2 "Census Profile 2016, Markham, Ontario," Statistics Canada, last modified August 9, 2019, http://www12.statcan.ca/census-recensement/2016/dp-pd/prof/details/page.cfm?Lang=E&Geo1=CSD&Code1=3519036&Geo2=PR&Code2=35&PR=01&B1=All&GeoLevel=PR&GeoCode=3519036.

3 Mark Suster, "73.6% of All Statistics Are Made up," *Business Insider*, February 17, 2010, https://www.businessinsider.com/736-of-all-statistics-are-made-up-2010-2.

4 "Population Estimates on July 1, by Age and Sex," Statistics Canada, last modified February 13, 2020, http://www.statcan.gc.ca/tables-tableaux/sum-som/l01/cst01/demo10a-eng.htm.

5   "What is Intersex?" Intersex Society of North America, last modified 2008, http://www.isna.org/faq/what_is_intersex.

6   "How Common Is Intersex?" Intersex Society of North America, last modified 2008, http://www.isna.org/faq/frequency.

7   Michael T. Robinson, "Which Generation Are You?" Career Planner, accessed February 13, 2020, https://www.careerplanner.com/Career-Articles/Generations.cfm.

8   "21.9% of Canadians Are Immigrants, the Highest Share in 85 Years: Statscan," CBC, October 25, 2017, https://www.cbc.ca/news/politics/census-2016-immigration-1.4368970.

9   "A Profile of Persons with Disabilities among Canadians Aged 15 Years or Older, 2012," Statistics Canada, last modified February 15, 2017, http://www.statcan.gc.ca/pub/89-654-x/89-654-x2015001-eng.htm.

10   "Federal Disability Reference Guide," Government of Canada, last modified August 5, 2013, https://www.canada.ca/en/employment-social-development/programs/disability/arc/reference-guide.html.

11   "Persons with Disabilities and Employment," Statistics Canada, last modified November 27, 2015, https://www.statcan.gc.ca/pub/75-006-x/2014001/article/14115-eng.htm.

12   U.S. Bureau of Labor Statistics, "Persons with a Disability: Labor Force Characteristics Summary," news release no. USDL-20-0339, Wednesday, February 26, 2020, https://www.bls.gov/news.release/disabl.nr0.htm.

13   "Aboriginal Peoples in Canada: Key Results from the 2016 Census," Statistics Canada, last modified July 2, 2019, http://www.statcan.gc.ca/daily-quotidien/171025/dq171025a-eng.htm. Note that, in Canada, the term "Aboriginal," referring to First Nations, Inuit, and Metis people, has largely been replaced with "Indigenous."

14   "Immigration and Ethnocultural Diversity: Key Results from the 2016 Census," Statistics Canada, last modified November 1, 2017, http://www.statcan.gc.ca/daily-quotidien/171025/dq171025b-eng.htm.

15   Kathryn Blaze Carlson, "The True North LGBT: New Poll Reveals
     Landscape of Gay Canada," *National Post*, July 6, 2012, http://national-
     post.com/news/canada/the-true-north-lgbt-new-poll-reveals-landscape-
     of-gay-canada.

16   Frank Newport, "In U.S., Estimate of LGBT Population Rises to 4.5%,"
     Gallup, May 22, 2018, https://news.gallup.com/poll/234863/esti-
     mate-lgbt-population-rises.aspx?g_source=link_NEWSV9&g_medium=
     TOPIC&g_campaign=item_&g_content=In%2520U.S.%2c%2520Esti
     mate%2520of%2520LGBT%2520Population%2520Rises%
     2520to%25204.5%2525.

17   Thomas Sasso and Amy Ellard-Gray, *In and Out: Diverging Perspectives on
     LGBT Inclusion in the Workplace*, CCDI, 2015, http://ccdi.ca/
     media/1070/20150528-report-lgbt-inclusion-in-the-workplace-en.pdf.

18   "Census Profile 2016, Markham, Ontario," Statistics Canada, last
     modified August 9, 2019, https://www12.statcan.gc.ca/census-
     recensement/2016/dp-pd/prof/index.cfm?Lang=E.

19   "Data Profiles 2016," American Community Survey, United States
     Census Bureau, https://www.census.gov/acs/www/data/data-tables-
     and-tools/data-profiles/2016/.

20   Rhian Daly, "Reebok Slams 'Categorically False' Reports Beyoncé
     Walked out of Deal over Diversity Row," NME, April 8, 2019, https://
     www.nme.com/news/music/beyonce-reportedly-turned-down-reebok-deal-
     2473159.

21   "By 2050, U.S. Could Have More Spanish Speakers Than Any Country,"
     LanguageLine Solutions Blog, August 12, 2019, accessed March 29,
     2020, https://blog.languageline.com/by-2050-u.s.-could-have-more-spanish-
     speakers-than-any-country.

22   "20 Advantages and Disadvantages of Diversity in the Workplace,"
     Future of Working: The Leadership and Career Blog, accessed February
     13, 2020, https://futureofworking.com/11-advantages-and-disadvantages-
     of-diversity-in-the-workplace/.

23   Deloitte Australia and the Victorian Equal Opportunity and Human
     Rights Commission, "Waiter, Is That Inclusion In My Soup? A New
     Recipe to Improve Business Performance," May 2013, https://www2.
     deloitte.com/content/dam/Deloitte/au/Documents/human-capital/deloitte-au-hc-
     diversity-inclusion-soup-0513.pdf.

24 Vivian Hunt, Dennis Layton, and Sara Prince, *Diversity Matters*, McKinsey and Company, February 2, 2015. https://www.mckinsey.com/~/media/mckinsey/business%20functions/organization/our%20insights/why%20diversity%20matters/diversity%20matters.ashx.

25 Vivian Hunt, Dennis Layton, and Sara Prince, "Why Diversity Matters," McKinsey and Company, January 2015, https://www.mckinsey.com/business-functions/organization/our-insights/why-diversity-matters.

26 Vivian Hunt, Sara Prince, Sundiatu Dixon-Fyle, and Lareina Yee, *Delivering Through Diversity*, McKinsey and Company, January 2018, https://www.mckinsey.com/~/media/McKinsey/Business%20Functions/Organization/Our%20Insights/Delivering%20through%20diversity/Delivering-through-diversity_full-report.ashx.

27 "Policy on Removing the 'Canadian Experience' Barrier," Ontario Human Rights Commissions, February 1, 2013, http://www.ohrc.on.ca/en/policy-removing-%E2%80%9Ccanadian-experience%E2%80%9D-barrier.

28 CCDI, *Locking in Your Leadership: Developing the Ironclad Business Case for D&I*, January 20, 2014, https://ccdi.ca/media/2082/20200130-locking-in-your-leadership-toolkit-for-developing-the-ironclad-business-case-for-di.pdf.

Chapter 4: The Right Way to Do Diversity

1 Ibid.

2 *Oxford Dictionary*, s.v. "change management (n.)," accessed February 13, 2020, https://www.lexico.com/en/definition/change_management.

3 "Everyone Loves Progress—Nobody Likes Change," First American Professional Real Estate Services, accessed February 13, 2020, http://www.firstamprs.com/content/everyone-loves-progress-nobody-likes-change.

Chapter 6: Attracting Difference

1 Jeffrey Dastin, "Amazon Scraps Secret AI Recruiting Tool That Showed Bias against Women," Reuters, Technology News, October 9, 2018, https://www.reuters.com/article/us-amazon-com-jobs-automation-in-sight/amazon-scraps-secret-ai-recruiting-tool-that-showed-bias-against-women-idUSKCN1MK08G.

2 Curt Rice, "How Blind Auditions Help Orchestras to Eliminate Gender Bias," *Guardian*, October 14, 2014, https://www.theguardian.com/women-in-leadership/2013/oct/14/blind-auditions-orchestras-gender-bias.

3 "Policy on Removing the 'Canadian Experience' Barrier," Ontario Human Rights Commission, February 1, 2013, http://www.ohrc.on.ca/en/policy-removing-%E2%80%9Ccanadian-experience%E2%80%9D-barrier.

Chapter 7: Developing Your People

1 Linda Babcock and Sara Laschever, *Women Don't Ask: Negotiation and the Gender Divide* (New York: Bantam Dell, 2007).

2 Susan Cain, *Quiet: The Power of Introverts in a World that Can't Stop Talking* (New York: Crown Publishers, 2012), 10–11.

3 Gordon C. Nagayama Hall, "The Platinum Rule," *Psychology Today*, February 7, 2017, https://www.psychologytoday.com/ca/blog/life-in-the-intersection/201702/the-platinum-rule.

Chapter 8: Measurement for Success

1 Julie O'Mara and Alan Richter, Global Diversity and Inclusion Benchmarks: Standards for Organizations Around the World, The Centre for Global Inclusion, 2017, p. 43, http://centreforglobalinclusion.org/wp-content/uploads/2017/09/GDIB-V.09517.pdf.

2 Ben Jonson, *Every Man in His Humour*, 1598.

3 CCDI, *Diversity by the Numbers: The Legal Profession*, November 30, 2016, p. 33, https://ccdi.ca/attachments/DBTN_TLP_2016.pdf.

4   "Gender Wage Gap," OECD, Data, accessed February 13, 2020, https://data.oecd.org/earnwage/gender-wage-gap.htm.

5   Encyclopedia of Research Design, s.v. "triangulation," accessed February 13, 2020, https://methods.sagepub.com/Reference//encyc-of-research-design/n469.xml.

6   Deloitte Australia and the Victorian Equal Opportunity and Human Rights Commission, "Waiter, Is That Inclusion in My Soup?"

7   "Falling Employee Engagement 'Wake-Up Call' for Employers: Survey," Canadian HRReporter, March 14, 2018, https://www.hrreporter.com/focus-areas/culture-and-engagement/falling-employee-engagement-wake-up-call-for-employers-survey/283066.

8   According to a study by Gallup, organizations with high levels of employee engagement saw a 21 percent increase in productivity. See Susan Sorenson, "How Employee Engagement Drives Growth," Gallup, Workplace, June 20, 2013, https://www.gallup.com/workplace/236927/employee-engagement-drives-growth.aspx.

9   Shane Hall, "What Is the Average Worker's Effective Productivity Rate?" Chron, accessed February 13, 2020, https://smallbusiness.chron.com/average-workers-effective-productivity-rate-18220.html.

Chapter 9: The Key Ingredients

1   Sujay Vardhmane, *Diversity and Inclusion Councils: Toolkit for Diversity and Inclusion Practitioners*, CCDI, September 2017, https://ccdi.ca/media/1072/20170831-ccdi-diversity-council-toolkit-final-v3.pdf.

2   Ethan S. Bernstein and Stephen Turban, "The Impact of the 'Open' Workspace on Human Collaboration," *Philosophical Transactions of the Royal Society B, Biological Sciences* 373, no. 1753 (August 9, 2018), https://doi.org/10.1098/rstb.2017.0239.

3   Rebekah Bastian, "How to Foster Workplace Belonging Through Successful Employee Resource Groups," Forbes, February 11, 2019, https://www.forbes.com/sites/rebekahbastian/2019/02/11/how-to-foster-workplace-belonging-through-successful-employee-resource-groups/#759aaf21dc73.

4   CCDI, *Employee Resource Groups: Toolkit for Diversity and Inclusion Practitioners*, July 16, 2015, https://ccdi.ca/media/1073/20150716-ccdi-report-erg-toolkit.pdf.

5   "There Is More to D&I Than Meets the Eye," Office of Economic Impact and Diversity, Employee Resource Groups, accessed February 13, 2020, https://www.energy.gov/diversity/services/diversity-and-inclusion/ employee-resource-groups.

6   The Arquives: Canada's LGBTQ2+ Archives, s.v. "Gay and Lesbian Organization of Bell Employees (GLOBE) fonds," accessed February 13, 2020, https://arquives.andornot.com/en/permalink/descriptions22631.

7   Ibid.

8   CCDI, *Employee Resource Groups*.

9   CCDI, *Canadian Certified Inclusion Professional Competency Framework*, 2018, https://ccdi.ca/media/1708/20180409-competency-frame-work-v11.pdf.

Chapter 10: From the Leading Edge to the Bleeding Edge

1   "Accessibility Guidelines Working Group," W3C Web Accessibility Initiative (WAI), accessed February 13, 2020, https://www.w3.org/WAI/GL/.

2   Nick Wolny, "The LGBTQ+ Community Has $3.7 Trillion In Purchasing Power; Here's How We Want You to Sell to Us," *Entrepreneur*, June 10, 2019, https://www.entrepreneur.com/article/334983.

3   Graeme McMillan, "It's Not You, It's It: Voice Recognition Doesn't Recognize Women," *Time*, Accessories and Peripherals, June 1, 2011, http://techland.time.com/2011/06/01/its-not-you-its-it-voice-recognition-doesnt-recognize-women/.

4   Robert Rodriguez, "Diversity Finds Its Place," SHRM, August 1, 2006, https://www.shrm.org/hr-today/news/hr-magazine/pages/0806rodriguez.aspx.

Chapter 11: White Man Trumps All

1   "Are You in Favour of Same-Sex Marriage? 74% of Canadians and 80% of Quebecers Support It," CROP, November 20, 2017, https://www.crop.ca/en/blog/2017/207/.

2   Éric Grenier, "Conflicted and Worried: CBC News Poll Takes Snapshot of
     Canadians Ahead of Fall Election," CBC News, Politics, June 30, 2019,
     https://www.cbc.ca/news/politics/cbc-election-poll-1.5188097.

3   Ibid.

4   "Prime Minister Announces Special Advisor on LGBTQ2 Issues," Justin
     Trudeau, Prime Minister of Canada, November 15, 2016, https://pm.gc.
     ca/eng/news/2016/11/15/prime-minister-announces- special-advisor-
     lgbtq2-issues.

5   John Kalbfleisch, "Quebec, 1944: Finally, Women Are Allowed to Vote,"
     Montreal Gazette, September 7, 2012, https://www.montrealgazette.
     com/life/Quebec+1944+Finally+women+allowed+vote/7185694/
     story.html.

6   John C. Courtney, The Canadian Encyclopedia online, s.v. "Right to Vote
     in Canada," last modified February 15, 2019, https://www.the
     canadianencyclopedia.ca/en/article/franchise.

7   "The Facts about the Gender Wage Gap in Canada," Canadian Women's
     Foundation, accessed February 13, 2020, https://canadianwomen.org/
     the-facts/the-wage-gap-2/.

8   Caroline Kelley, "'It Won't Work': Kamala Harris' Campaign Slams
     Online Attacks on Her Race," CNN, Politics, June 30, 2019, https://www.
     cnn.com/2019/06/29/politics/kamala-harris-responds-donald-trump-jr-
     race-african-american-black/index.html.

9   Wikipedia, s.v. "Oppression Olympics," last modified March 21, 2020,
     https://en.wikipedia.org/wiki/Oppression_Olympics.

10 Dictionary.com, s.v. "white guilt (n.)," accessed February 13, 2020,
     https://www.dictionary.com/browse/white-guilt.

11 Judith H. Katz, White Awareness: Handbook for Anti-Racism Training
     (Norman: University of Oklahoma Press, 1978, 2003).

12 Oxford Dictionary, s.v. "privilege (n.)," accessed February 13, 2020,
     https://www.lexico.com/en/definition/privilege.

13 Megan Gannon, "Race Is a Social Construct, Scientists Argue," Scientific
     American, LiveScience (blog), February 5, 2016, https://www.

scientificamerican.com/article/race-is-a-social-construct-
scientists-argue/.

Chapter 12: Overcoming Diversity Fatigue

1   *Oxford Dictionary*, s.v. "fatigue (*n.*)," accessed February 13, 2020, https://
www.lexico.com/en/definition/fatigue.

2   "Self-Help Tips to Fight Tiredness," National Health Service, accessed
February 13, 2020, https://www.nhs.uk/live-well/sleep-and-tiredness/
self-help-tips-to-fight-fatigue/.

3   Melissa Conrad Stoppler, "Endorphins: Natural Pain and Stress Fighters,"
MedicineNet, June 13, 2018, https://www.medicinenet.com/endorphins_
natural_pain_and_stress_fighters/views.htm.

4   Kevin B. Hendricks and Vinod R. Singhal, "Quality Awards and the
Market Value of the Firm," *Management Science* 42, no. 3 (March 1996),
https://doi.org/10.1287/mnsc.42.3.415.

Chapter 13: What Gets in the Way?

1   *Oxford Dictionary*, s.v. "self-interest (*n.*)," accessed February 13, 2020,
https://www.lexico.com/en/definition/self-interest.

2   Éric Grenier, "Canadians are Worried about Climate Change, but Many
Don't Want to Pay Taxes to Fight It," CBC News, Politics, June 18, 2019,
https://www.cbc.ca/news/politics/election-poll-climate-change-
1.5178514.

3   Philip Authier, "Bill 21: Quebec Passes Secularism Law after Marathon
Session," *Montreal Gazette*, June 18, 2019, https://montrealgazette.com/
news/quebec/quebec-passes-secularism-law-after-marathon-session.

4   "Exposure to Chemicals in Plastic," Breastcancer.org, accessed February
13, 2020, https://www.breastcancer.org/risk/factors/plastic.

Michael Bach is nationally and internationally recognized as a thought leader and subject matter expert in the fields of diversity, equity, and inclusion, and he brings a vast knowledge of leading practices in a live setting to his work. He is the CEO of the Canadian Centre for Diversity and Inclusion, an organization that he founded in 2012 with the mandate of helping to educate Canadians on the value of diversity and inclusion. CCDI operates in eighteen cities across Canada, as well as around the world, helping employers create inclusive workplaces. Under Michael's leadership, the organization has received numerous awards, including the *Canadian HR Reporter*'s Readers' Choice Award in the category of Diversity/Employment Equity Consultant from 2016 to 2019.

Prior to founding CCDI, he was the national director of Diversity, Equity and Inclusion for KPMG in Canada, a role he created and held for seven years. Additionally, Michael completed a two-and-a-half-year secondment as the deputy chief diversity officer for KPMG International. During his tenure, KPMG (Canada) received several prestigious diversity-related awards, including being named one of Canada's Top Employers for Diversity and one of Canada's Best Employers for New Canadians.

Over the course of his career, Michael has received repeated recognition for his work, including being named as one of the Women of Influence's 2012 Canadian Diversity Champions. In 2011 he was honored as the Diversity Champion with the Catalyst Canada Honours Human Resources/Diversity Leader award. He also received the Women of Influence's 2011 Canadian Diversity Champions award, the 2011 Inspire Award as LGBTQ Person of the Year, and the 2011 Out on Bay Street (now called Start Proud) Leaders to be Proud of LGBT Advocate Workplace Award. In 2010 Michael was honored by the Toronto Immigrant Employment Council with the 2010 IS Award Canadian HR Reporter Individual Achievement Award.

Michael has a post-graduate certificate in diversity management from Cornell University, and he also holds the Cornell Certified Diversity Professional, Advanced Practitioner (CCDP/AP) designation.